Mountain Musings

Mountain Musings

A Collection of Short Stories

GENE VICKERS

Mountain Arbor
Press
Alpharetta, GA

ISBN: 978-1-6653-0095-7 0 2 2 2 2 2

♾This paper meets the requirements of ANSI/NISO Z39.48-1992 (Permanence of Paper)

To Beth

Life is full of short stories and all
one has to do is look around to see them.

—Gene Vickers

Contents

Section 3

INTRODUCTION

I have often viewed my life as an assortment of stories. Some have been happy ones, and some have been sad. It takes both kinds to make us appreciate life as a whole. I've been writing short stories for many years, and the ones in this book are a sampling of my work. I put together a selection of stories to give you a look into the world as I see it, where anything and everything can fit comfortably into a story. I hope you enjoy the book.

The first section uses humor and anthropomorphism to engage the reader. The stories will share what a turtle knows about Clint Eastwood, what to do when your wife says "jump", and the difference between houseflies and restaurant flies. You'll experience the reality of being trapped in iPad hell, and get the inside details of what really happened when the prodigal son returned home.

The second section of *Mountain Musings* incorporates faith and family values with delightful and engaging stories. Find out about the first miracle, what Christmas did to the old rental house and how one might count their blessings. One of the greatest commandments is highlighted, and a father takes a look into life's rear-view mirror.

The last section is more thought-provoking, allowing the reader to feel the depth of true love and sacrifice, the emotions of an empty nest and the hopelessness someone feels when they lose their family and job. Experience the tragedy of a hit and run accident or spend some time with the old man and the bee.

Section 1

FREE-RANGE HOUSE CHICKENS

Sara had enrolled in Continuing Education classes at the local college. The ones she found most interesting were those on nutrition. Ed, her husband, had high cholesterol and was a borderline diabetic. A teacher in one of the nutrition classes convinced Sara that she could fix all of her husband's health issues by simply changing the types of food they were eating and how she prepared their meals.

Sara and Ed had no children. They had a Boston Terrier named Cooper, or Coopdog for short. Ed loved that dog as much as some people love their children. When Ed was home, Coopdog was always with him.

Ed, a traveling salesman, would leave home on Monday and usually return by Thursday or Friday. Scheduled to be home on Friday, Ed finished early one week, so he came home late

Thursday night, with the intention of surprising Sara. He didn't call, and she was already in bed and asleep when Ed came into the house. He had bought her a surprise gift and was hoping she would still be up so he could give it to her.

In the laundry room, he quietly removed his socks and shoes. The big surprise was not the one he had in his hand for his wife. It was the surprise Sara had for him, and it was on the kitchen floor. Without turning on a light, he walked barefoot across the kitchen. Stepping in something, he felt it squish up between his toes. Unable to imagine what it was, he immediately turned on the kitchen light.

"My God," Ed yelled at the top of his lungs. He was eyeball to eyeball with four large chickens sitting on the island counter. He was the proverbial fox in the hen house. The chickens flailed the air with their wings and squawked as loud as chickenly possible. The commotion scared Sara silly. She let out a blood-curdling scream from their bedroom. Ed could hear wings flapping in other parts of the house. As he looked down on the floor, there weren't many safe places to step.

Sara came flying into the kitchen. "What are you doing home?" she asked, as if he had committed a crime by coming home early.

"Stepping in chicken poop and waking the chickens up, I guess would be a fair answer."

"Watch where you step!"

"No kidding," Ed said as if he had thought about trying to walk any farther.

In utter disbelief, Ed surveyed the barnyard scene that had previously been their kitchen.

"I can explain," Sara said quickly. "I wasn't expecting you until Friday evening, and I had hoped to get all the chickens and the rooster house-broken by then. They've been doing really well all week, and the scare you just gave them will probably cause them to have a setback."

"A setback! A setback! You're concerned about these chickens having a setback. I'm standing here knee-deep in chicken poop, and you're accusing me of traumatizing a bunch of chickens in a house-breaking session. Our beautiful kitchen; what have you done to our beautiful kitchen?"

Ed's facial expression was somewhere between disbelief and horror. Running both hands through his hair and grabbing a handful, Ed thought about screaming at the top of his lungs.

Sara knew she was knee-deep in a dilemma of her own making.

"Since I already have my toes in it, let's see if I can wrap my mind around it as well. The chickens have been here for the whole time I've been gone?"

"And the rooster. He arrived the same day the chickens did."

"And the rooster; heaven forbid we forget about the rooster. Does this rooster have a name, so I can address him properly in case I see him? Surely you have named the rooster by now. After all, he's been living with you in our house for a whole week."

"As a matter of fact, he does have a name. The farmer that sold him to me said his name was Roy. And the reason you haven't seen Roy is because he prefers the upstairs bedroom for sleeping. But I'm sure you woke him up as well. You woke me and all of the chickens. Why would I think Roy was able to sleep through your grand entrance?"

"Grand entrance indeed," Ed said sarcastically. "I'm sure Queen Elizabeth always finds chicken poop between her toes whenever she makes one of her grand entrances. And by the way, where's my dog?

"Our dog!"

"No! My dog. Apparently you now have chickens, and lots of them. And let's not forget about fun-loving Roy who sleeps in the guest bedroom upstairs because he prefers it over the lowly first-floor accommodations. And, where is Coopdog?"

"He's in our bedroom, in his crate."

"And why is he in the crate. He hates that crate."

"Not anymore. He actually likes the crate now."

"I'm almost afraid to ask, but why does Coopdog like the crate now?"

"He's afraid of Roy. Now, Roy doesn't bother him, not really. He just likes to play chase with him. Roy pretends he's going to peck him, and that causes Coopdog to run."

Ed headed for the bedroom to free an imprisoned Coopdog. The reunion was heart-warming. If Coopdog could speak, he would have told Ed he ran from Roy because Roy was twice as big as he was. And, as for pretending to peck him, he would have also told Ed to examine the plugs Roy had taken out of his butt. No pretending there. Ed held Coopdog like a mother holds her precious baby. The minute they left the bedroom and the safety of the crate, Coopdog began to shake. And at the sight of the first chicken in the living room, he began to whimper and whine.

"My God, Sara, what have you done to this poor dog? He's terrified. We'll talk in the morning. And it'll be a serious conversation. Coopdog and I are going to the basement. Please tell me no newly adopted feathered family members are in my basement."

"There are no chickens in our basement. The farmer said it would be too dark and would affect their egg production. After the scare you gave them, they'll probably never lay eggs again."

Ed reached over and turned out the kitchen light.

"Why did you do that?"

"I think my chances are better in the dark. I'll probably step in less that way than if I try and step around and over it. If they've made improvements on being house-broken, I can't imagine what the floor looked like on Tuesday. Good night, Sara."

Ed went to the basement and took a shower. Coopdog stood outside the shower and trembled. It took more than an hour before he started to relax. He jumped every time one of the feathered guest upstairs flapped a wing or made any sort of chicken sounds.

With flapping and clucking as background music, it took Ed forever to fall asleep. He kept visualizing his toes and the floor in the kitchen.

Morning came early as Roy did his thing in the upstairs bedroom.

"I have died and gone to barnyard hell," Ed thought to himself as Roy blazed away with his wake-up call.

Coopdog was asleep, nestled up next to Ed when Roy went off. He jumped up with a look of sheer panic on his face as if trying to decide which way to run.

"Don't worry, boy." Ed picked him up to calm him. "Until I find out what Farmer Sara is up to, the basement is totally yours. Any chickens, and especially fun-loving Roy, finding their way down here will find themselves on our plate. And, if it happens to be Roy, you can have your choice as to which pieces you want to eat. How does that sound, Coopdog?"

Ed and Coopdog were close. It seemed to Ed his canine friend understood what he was told. He wagged his tail, if you consider how a Boston Terrier wags what's left of his tail, in what seemed to Ed as appreciation for the sanctity of the basement and the promise of fresh chicken, preferably fresh rooster, on his plate.

As Ed started to get dressed, he remembered the "stuff" that had oozed up between his toes last evening. It made him shudder all over and another shower was in order. Talk about a foot-washing service; the disciples didn't have anything on Ed. Again, Coopdog stood outside the shower and trembled.

"Don't worry, Coopdog," Ed reassured him. "I'll have a summit conference shortly with Farmer Sara and find out if she remembers where she lost her mind and I'll try and help her locate it. It's clear to me that insanity is the culprit here. No one in their right mind would turn chickens loose in their home."

At the sound of the word chickens, Coopdog started to shake again. Ed turned on the radio, put it on a classical music station and turned the volume up enough to cover up any barnyard sounds originating upstairs. Ed called out to Sara, who quickly came to the door of the basement.

"What?" Sara asked with both hands on her hips. She expected the confrontation they were about to have would be unpleasant, to say the least.

"Let's go out and get some breakfast," Ed said softly, so as not to disturb Coopdog. "We need to talk and work out something with Animal Farm. Think Orwell could help?"

Sara didn't think the Orwell comment was funny.

"I can't leave the free-range house chickens right now. I have to get them outside in the fenced-in area so they can feed and potty."

"Based on the accumulation on the kitchen floor, I wouldn't think they would need to potty again for at least another week. Wait a minute," Ed said. Sara's remark had sunk in. "Did you say fenced-in area as with wire and posts and such? Fenced-in area!!!"

"Ed, I'm doing every bit of this for you. My nutrition teacher says the eggs from free-range house chickens are great for your overall well-being. They are full of—,"

"Did you say fenced-in area, in my backyard?"

"It's our backyard, and yes I did."

Sara descended the steps and had walked over to the basement door leading to the backyard.

"Now don't get upset, Ed," Sara said.

"My God, Sara, what have you done to my yard and all of my beautiful landscaping?"

A six-foot tall fence made of chicken wire enclosed Ed's entire back yard. Bales of hay had been strewn here and there for the chickens and cornstalks littered the ground. All of Ed's plants had been destroyed by the chickens scratching in the flower beds.

"Why did you do this?" Ed asked. "Our backyard was so beautiful."

"It was a package deal, Ed. My teacher's brother put together a free-range house chicken package that included thirty free-range house chickens."

"Thirty chickens! There are thirty chickens in my house?"

"Ed, it's our house, and if you'll stop interrupting, I'll tell you about the great deal the farmer, who's the nutrition teacher's brother, gave us."

"He didn't give us anything. He fleeced you and made you like it because he's in cahoots with that phony teacher of yours."

"Okay, Ed, enough with the accusations and sarcasm. Do you want to hear what I got in the package deal or not?"

"I can't wait," Ed responded as he stared shell-shocked at his backyard.

"I'll try again. Thirty free-range house chickens, feed troughs, watering troughs, hay bales, cornstalks, free-range feed plots and the six-foot fenced-in backyard using pressure-treated posts. There's also a coupon that allows us to buy thirty more free-range house chickens at a discount of twenty-five percent off."

"You forgot one thing," Ed said, staring at his backyard as if in a catatonic state.

"And what might that be?" Sara asked.

"Roy, fun-loving Roy, wake up the world Roy."

"I didn't forget Roy. Roy wasn't part of the package. He was extra. We got a real bargain, Ed.

The entire free-range house chicken setup, including the discount coupon that will allow us to buy thirty more free-range house chickens, was only $1800.00. And Roy; Roy was $175.00. He's a special rooster because he has always been a free-ranger. Those are real hard to find and the farmer was reluctant to sell him."

Ed was hyper-ventilating when he went back into the basement. He picked Coopdog up and noticed his hair was falling out. The trauma was simply too much.

Ed moved all of his personal belongings to the basement, everything except his alarm clock. Fun-loving Roy could wake the dead from his second-story bedroom. No need to ever set the alarm clock again.

Four weeks to the day after Sara bought the free-range house chickens, Coopdog was completely hairless—a naked Boston Terrier with the shakes and pock marks on his butt. He never went into the backyard again. One day, he went out in the front yard to potty and never returned. Ed couldn't find him anywhere. He simply left Ed and the free-range house chicken ranch.

A week after Coopdog left, Ed left as well. He had been gone two weeks before Sara even missed him. She filed a missing person's report, but it didn't do any good. Both Ed and Coopdog had just vanished.

Sara was so busy she didn't miss either one of them. She had special lighting installed in the basement and bought the deluxe free-range house chicken package that came with seventy-five free range house chickens and a free rooster. She soon had eggs to sell.

From time to time, someone would spot a hairless Boston Terrier running around the neighborhood. A friend of the family told Sara he'd made a delivery to the poultry processing plant and had seen a man who looked just like Ed killing chickens. He went on to say it couldn't be Ed because he knew Ed well enough to know that he could never kill chickens. It had to be someone who just looked like him.

When the insurance company paid off on Ed's life insurance policy, Sara went big time and bought two hundred and fifty acres. She also bought 2,500 free range chickens and an adequate supply of roosters. She has over 20 employees and is selling free-range house-chicken franchises via the internet.

The only feathered one actually in Sara's new home is fun-loving Roy. He is no longer the trusted trumpeter of the morning. He's stuffed and sits on a pedestal inside Sara's posh office. Coopdog would love to see that!

iPAD HELL

Two deputies from the sheriff's department and two paramedics had responded to the call at 4819 Blankenship Road. The coroner had been called and everyone was waiting for him. One of the deputies was trying to get a statement from Mrs. Johnson, the wife of the deceased.

"Ma'am, when did you first notice your husband had passed away?" Deputy Edge asked as sensitively as possible.

"Well, I guess it was around–" Her iPad alerted her to an incoming message and she said, "Excuse me, sir. Let me see who this is."

The deputy nodded and lowered his clipboard to his side while Mrs. Johnson was checking out her recent message. Mr. Johnson was in a recliner, covered with a sheet from the ambulance.

"Sir," Mrs. Johnson said excitedly. "You won't believe who just sent me a message on my iPad. I've been trying to locate this rascal for nearly two months. I went to grammar school with him, and we were in the second grade together. Let's see. That would make it about sixty-eight years ago. I was about to give up on finding him. Figured he had probably passed by now. Lots of them have, you know."

"Yes, ma'am," the officer responded to the grammar school update. "I really need to get this report filled out before the coroner gets here. It'll save him a lot of time if we already have the information recorded. When do you think Mr. Johnson passed?"

Another alert, and she immediately skirted the question again.

"Why, that little stinker just sent me a picture. His name is Jimmy Smith, but we always called him Little Jimmy. Wanna know why? Because he was so short. Some of the girls could pick him up and carry him around like a doll. Used to make him so mad. Come here, officer. You gotta see this. He hasn't changed a bit. Looks just like he did in second grade."

Realizing he wasn't going to get his question answered until he took a peek at Little Jimmy, he walked over to the matching recliner Mrs. Johnson was sitting in. Peering over his glasses, the deputy saw a bald-headed old man, standing with the aid of a walker and smiling big time for the picture. The smile failed to display teeth, only gums.

"I swear," Mrs. Johnson said excitedly. "I know you didn't know him in the second grade like I did, but this picture is the spitting image of what I remember."

Deputy Edge smiled and said "Yes, ma'am. I'm sure you're right about that." He really wanted to say, "You've gotta be kidding me. No one, I mean no one, looks like that in the second grade." But instead he asked the same question a third time. "Now when did you first realize your husband was dead?"

She seemed preoccupied with her iPad again. "Hold on a second. Let me put this on Facebook. Won't take long. There's a bunch of my friends who have been looking for Little Jimmy and they'll be happy to know I found him."

After posting her find, she came back to the question.

"I'm sorry, officer, but that was important and I appreciate you letting me post it. Now, as to when I realized Frank had passed. Let's see now. Yesterday morning, I asked him if he wanted breakfast, but he didn't answer. He was sleeping up a storm. He plays a lot of those computer games and sometimes stays up half the night. Just sleeps right there in his recliner. I had lunch with some friends and then went to a movie with them. Last evening when I came home he was still in his recliner, taking a nap. He takes lots of naps. Calls them power naps."

Realizing activity had taken place on her iPad, she politely said, "Excuse me." After reading the post, she announced to the deputy that a close friend stumped her little toe and had posted a picture of how bruised and swollen it was. "Let me post a quick comment."

Deputy Edge marveled that a friend's stumped toe trumped a dead husband, covered up with a sheet, in a matching recliner, fifteen feet away from her.

"There," she said. "A stumped toe might not seem important, but it is to the one who's got it. It'll make her feel better to know I care. Now, where were we?"

"Last evening, you came in and Mr. Johnson was asleep in his chair," Deputy Edge reminded her.

"Yes, that's right, Frank was asleep in his chair. I tried not to wake him, went to our bedroom, put on my pajamas and got in bed to check my emails and to post my day's activities on Facebook."

"Can you remember seeing Mr. Johnson doing anything at all yesterday?"

"No, I can't, come to think of it. This morning, I got up and realized Frank had slept in his chair again. So, I took a picture of him with my iPad and posted it on Facebook. A friend of ours immediately sent me a private message and said Frank didn't look too well to her, kinda swollen and bluish around the lips. I sent her a message and told her I thought she might be right and then that's when I found out. I got out of my chair and went over and touched him. He was cold as ice. That's when I called 911."

"What did you do then?" Officer Edge asked.

"Frank didn't do Facebook, but we had lots of mutual friends. I took a few close-ups and posted them, so everyone would know I've lost my dear Frank and am in mourning."

"Thank you, ma'am, for your help. The coroner just pulled up and we'll be removing Mr. Johnson's body shortly. Sorry for your loss." Mrs. Johnson didn't hear a word Deputy Edge said to her. She was busy on her iPad again.

When the coroner gave the okay to remove the body, Mrs. Johnson was quickly jolted back to reality as the paramedics rolled her husband by her chair. It should have been a very painful moment.

She said, "Stop. Stop right there. I want to get a picture to put on Facebook. Where's Deputy Edge?"

Someone called him and he came immediately into the room.

"Stand right there in the middle of the gurney," she instructed the deputy. "And each of you," she said, addressing the paramedics, "look this way and smile." After taking several pictures, she thanked them, returned to her chair and began posting them to her Facebook page.

Mr. Johnson was on his way to the morgue, and Mrs. Johnson was in mourning, trapped in iPad hell.

FLASHES

The only thing in our home more confused than I am is the heating and cooling system. The confusion exists because my wife's thermostat is either broken or severely impaired.

"Aren't you cold?" I sometimes ask.

"Oh, no. Feels great to me," she'll reply.

"Aren't you hot?" I'll ask.

"Not me, it's just perfect in here."

The only thing more problematic than the house is the car, a much smaller, more confined space. I'm either freezing to death or sweating like a prostitute in church. With my wife, there's no in between. One day, she exclaimed, "Wow, I feel like I'm in Jamaica." It was thirty degrees outside, but she still opened the front door to "cool off the room." Boy, did it ever cool off the room.

I considered filing for a divorce, citing irreconcilable temperatures. I figured I was willing to give up fifty percent of everything to stop the nonsense. When the lawyer told me it was half of everything, I changed my mind. Now, I just suffer in silence. Freezing to death or sweating like a prostitute in church—what's a fellow to do?

TURTLEPROMPTER

There are two sides to every story, and since the turtle isn't here, I'll tell the story. As we were leaving the post office, across from the college, my wife abruptly put on the brakes and said, "Look, a turtle. Do you want to get him out of the road?"

"Sure," I said, "before the poor thing gets run over."

Getting out, I walked around to the front of the truck. There he was, in the middle of our lane, inside his shell and oblivious to the traffic barely missing him. He didn't have his door completely shut, and I could see his head and his eyes. Even when I picked him up, he still didn't shut his door.

When I got back into the truck, my wife asked me what I was going to do with him.

"Take him to Bubba's," I told her. "I think there's something wrong with his door. Turtles usually shut their door tighter than Dick's hatband."

"Does Bubba work on turtle doors?" she asked in a serious manner.

"Bubba can fix anything," I told her, "but first we'll take him home and put him in the courtyard next to the goldfish pond. He might enjoy being there. He won't have to worry about getting run over, and there's plenty of room for him to explore and ramble around. I think turtles ramble a lot. They never seem to have a specific destination. Case in point—this turtle leaving the post office, trying to cross a busy street, and for what? Is he enrolled at the college?"

With the conclusion of my analysis of turtle travel, our turtle, the one with the door that wouldn't completely shut, became agitated. All four legs came out at the same time, and his two front feet latched onto my fingers. I could feel his sharp toenails digging into my hand.

"Wait a minute, little fellow," I told the turtle.

"Do not let him get away from you," my wife said excitedly, "or you'll have to drive this truck and hold the turtle at the same time."

"See what happens when you try and do a good deed. I wind up with a hysterical wife and a psycho turtle."

"That's it, I've had enough!"

I looked over at my wife, who was hugging the door glass while trying to drive the truck.

"Don't look at me," she said quickly, "it was the turtle who said that."

"I was wrong and I stand corrected. A psycho wife and a psycho turtle! How lucky can a man get?"

"Look, buddy," the turtle said with emphasis. "Your wife isn't the problem here, you are. She didn't snatch me up and turtle-nap me on the way to class; you did. No one wants to go live in your courtyard and befriend your goldfish."

"Going to class! You were on your way to class; a class, as in a class at the college? Let me see if I actually understand what's happening here. You had been to the post office to check for mail and were just crossing the street, on your way back to class, when I snatched you out of danger and saved your life?"

"You're finally getting the picture, finally," the turtle said exhibiting even more frustration and attitude, "except for the last part, where you pretend to be Clint Eastwood."

"What could you possibly know about Clint Eastwood?" I asked.

"A man has to know his limitations," the turtle responded, "and you have serious limitations."

"I will not tolerate this level of disrespect," I told the turtle.

"Turn this truck around and take him back to the college," I told my wife.

"To the college or to the post office?" she asked.

"The college," I snapped, "he's already been to the post office."

UNEXPECTED DISAPPOINTMENTS

It was mid-afternoon and the barnyard was alive with activity. The animals had, on their own accord, found their way back to the barn. This they did every evening, but not mid-afternoon. Something very important had happened and unexpected disappointments were about to visit them; at least two of them.

Rohoe, the resident busy-body duck, was quacking her head off. "Has anyone seen Junior? I hear he's back, but has anyone actually seen him? Has the Father seen him yet? Is he really back and is he going to stay? Oh, I hope so, I do hope so."

The barnyard animals loved Junior. He was totally useless to his Father and to the farm, but he had a soft spot for the animals and had always given them extra food and grain.

"Oh, he's back," Clover said. "I was grazing in the front field and saw him coming over the hill. When the Father saw him, he ran out to meet him and to welcome him home; quite a touching reunion."

Clover was the family milk cow and received preferential treatment. Her stall was twice as large as everyone else, and she was pampered and well-fed. She considered herself special, because twice a day she was given preferential treatment at milking time.

Laymore confirmed the sighting of Junior.

"He's definitely back. I saw him, too. But he looked terrible. He was dirty and his clothes were ragged; didn't look like the Junior that left here a while ago."

Laymore was an old chicken, way past her laying prime. The only reason she hadn't become dinner was because the family was afraid to eat her. She had a substantial loss of feathers and had some type of skin condition causing her considerable irritation. She was always rolling in the dirt and scratching herself.

Sara, the broken-down old plow horse, weighed in. Sara was useless around the farm, was blind in one eye and had problems with her memory. She often had to be reminded when it was time to go to the barn for the night.

"Junior's definitely back. I saw him and the Father go out to the pasture where Brother was mending the fence. Brother was very excited to see him. He was waving his arms in the air and shouting with joy. I've never seen Brother so excited. Usually he just works, and works, and works, and never seems to enjoy life like Junior did. Boy, was he happy today when Junior came back home."

Tabitha, the fatted calf, was last to speak. She had been napping and had missed half of the conversation. She was so over-fed she liked to lie around and take afternoon snoozes. She didn't have to graze like the other animals. The Father kept her in the barn and she was stall-fed for the most part.

"Oh, happy day," Tabitha said with glee. "I bet there's going to be a party. Know what that means everyone? Laughter and fun and when the Father and his family are happy, we usually get extra food and those who work get time off. Won't this be a grand evening? A party, a party, we're going to have a party."

Barook, the farm donkey, was the last animal to come in each evening. He didn't care much for the others. He was by far the most intelligent. He listened more than he talked, was somewhat arrogant, always blunt, and usually crude with his pronouncements on the others in the barnyard family. He claimed to be a direct descendant of the donkey Christ rode into Jerusalem, and a cousin to the donkey Mary rode to Bethlehem. Everyone, though he wasn't their friend or confidant, respected him for his wisdom and ability to discern what was happening, or about to happen on the farm.

Today, as usual, Barook was the last to enter the barn. Everyone was so happy and excited, and bubbly with conversation. Entering unnoticed, he stood silently in the shadows. Having heard most of the conversation, it was time to weigh in, and set the dumb animals straight. This was classic Barook.

"The Lord have pity on all of you if something ever happens to me. Listen up, and try to understand. Just try, okay. I also saw him come over the hill this afternoon. Unlike most of you, I listen more than I talk. I got close enough to hear their conversation and therefore, I know what's about to go down. Junior came home filthy, ragged, and has no money or means of support. He told Father he would be willing to feed and take care of us, if he would just allow him to return home."

"That's great," Rohoe said excitedly. "Junior will give us extra food"

"Hush, you idiot," Barook said without pause. "Brother isn't happy, as Sara reported earlier. Sara's blind in one eye and can't see out of the other. Brother is so mad at Junior's return, he's packing to leave, even as we speak. He's leaving and says he'll never return."

"Why is he mad about Junior coming home?" Clover asked.

"Because," Barook continued, "Junior's never worked a day in his life and has always taken advantage of the Father's goodness. He walked out on the family and us as well. He never cared for us. He spent time in the barn giving us extra food to hide from the responsibility of the farm. When he left, Father gave him his portion, and Brother stayed here dutifully and toiled and worked as hard as always. That's why Brother's mad. The Father welcomes Junior home with open arms, and Brother has nothing but contempt for Junior. So he's about to leave home forever. Even though Brother's leaving greatly saddens the Father and the family, there's to be a huge party tonight for Junior's safe return. The Father gave him new clothes and even gave Junior the family ring."

"Oh, happy day, oh, happy day," Tabitha said again with joyous glee. "There's going to be a party, a really big party."

As Tabitha happily danced around the barn, the other animals sensed the excitement and were about to shift into party mode with Tabitha.

Barook, always one for drama, stood silently for a few moments watching the frivolity and happiness being displayed by Tabitha and the other farm animals.

"Oh, Tabitha, oh, Tabitha," Barook said. "Guess who's going to be the guest of honor and the center piece of the party tonight?"

"I give up, oh do tell us, who, who, will get to be the guest of honor at the party? Tabitha asked excitedly.

All of the animals hushed and Barook motioned for them to come closer for this special tidbit of information. He loved suspense and intentionally played this out to the end. "I overheard the Father give special instructions to one of the hired men."

He paused until he got the desired reaction.

"What special instructions?" Laymore asked. "Do tell us. The suspense is killing us."

"Well, not quite all of us," Barook said with a slight smirk at how Laymore's question helped to heighten the announcement he was about to make.

It was so quiet in the barn you could have heard a mouse sneeze.

"I heard the Father tell the hired man to go and kill the fatted calf and to prepare it for the party."

"Oh, no," Clover said, "this can't be happening. Come here, precious Tabitha, come here. We must do something quick."

Barook watched the pandemonium as the group of friends dealt with his announcement of Tabitha's immediate demise. He decided it would be a good thing to leave a last thought with the group. He stamped the ground with his front hooves to get their attention.

"It's an unfortunate fact of life. There has always been, and will always be, unexpected disappointments."

As he turned to go, he saw Brother hurriedly approaching the barn. The other animals saw him as well, and immediately stopped talking.

"Where do you think you're going?" Brother said to Barook. "You're coming with me."

Taking Barook by the halter, he proceeded to load him down for the departure trip; the one with no return intended.

Instantly, they all remembered what would be Barook's last words of wisdom imparted to them just a few moments earlier.

"It's an unfortunate fact of life. There has always been, and will always be, unexpected disappointments."

POP SAYS

Don't let the white hair deceive you! I'm not a young man, and I'm sure as hell not your Pop. I can out walk you on most days and out work you any day of the week. You have no work ethic, no drive, and no respect for your elders. I get up every morning before you do, and your Mommy probably has to tuck you in at night, long before I lay down to sleep.

I've had successes in life people like you only dream about. I'll probably accomplish more with whatever time I have left than you will if you live to be a hundred.

So, young man, Pop has something to say to you. "KISS OFF!"

BIG BOB FROG

Big Bob Frog was king of the pond and ruler of Lily Pad. One day, as Tony Turtle passed by, he noticed Big Bob was sad and seemed very frustrated. This was unusual for Big Bob. He was always happy and easy-going.

"What's wrong Big Bob?" Tony Turtle asked, as he crawled slowly by.

"I've lost my contact lenses," Big Bob said, "and now I can't see anything. And, since I can't see, I can't eat, and right now I'm starving to death."

Tony Turtle didn't know what contact lenses were and really didn't care whether Big Bob could see or not see. As he crawled by a despondent Bob, he only had one thought, "If Big Bob can't see and therefore cannot eat, then there will be more food for me." That made Tony Turtle smile.

Bethy Wethy, the local pond snake came slithering by and found it quite amusing that Big Bob was crying. She had talked to Tony down at the dam and he had informed her that Big Bob was in a pickle, couldn't see, and therefore couldn't find anything to eat.

Bethy Wethy had a reputation for being blunt, and today it would be no different.

"Horse radishes," she told Big Bob, when she passed him at the other end of the pond. "Who cares if you can't see? That means that there will be more bugs and insects for everyone else in Lily Pad. You've always eaten more than your share and maybe you'll learn something about getting by on less like the rest of us. Might even be a good thing."

It was the talk of the pond and Lily Pad. Big Bob had always been a little bit on the pompous side and had no real friends. Anytime someone tried to befriend him, he would usually have a hunger pain sometime during the relationship and the new friend, if a bug or an insect, would disappear. Everyone at Lily Pad had to eat, but Bethy Wethy had indeed made a good observation. Big Bob ate for the sake of eating. Anything small enough for him to consume was usually eaten quickly. He ate far more than his share of bugs and insects.

Big Bob knew Bethy Wethy was right. No one would help him. The other frogs, turtles and snakes were excited about having more to eat. Why should anyone help Big Bob find his contact lenses? He was beside himself with frustration when he heard a tiny, small voice, speak to him.

"Good morning, sir, and how are you today?" the tiny, small voice asked.

Big Bob regained his composure, realizing the voice probably belonged to a tiny bug that was new to the pond and Lily Pad and was unaware of the reputation of the one he was addressing.

"I'm actually quite well," Big Bob told the tiny voice. "Things couldn't be any better. Well, maybe they could be a little better. I have a problem, not a big problem, it's really a very small problem, creating, well, you know, more of an inconvenience than anything else. Might I inquire as to the name of the one asking about my well-being?"

The tiny bug didn't answer. Big Bob thought for a moment that he had left. Another moment passed and still no response or sound from the passerby's tiny voice. Big Bob couldn't help himself and teared up again, overcome with emotion over his predicament.

"Are you crying?" asked the tiny voice. "And by the way, my friends call me Tiny Bug."

"Well, maybe I am, and maybe I'm not. Define crying, Tiny Bug," Big Bob said in an effort to strike up a conversation.

"Crying is something someone does to demand attention or remedy. Weeping or shedding tears is a way to achieve resolution to a given situation," Tiny Bug said, in a small, but intellectual voice.

Big Bob wasn't about to let his only chance of finding his contact lenses get away.

"That's quite a definition," Big Bob said. He was straining to see his new friend, but couldn't see anything smaller than the rock he was occupying. "Based on the definition you just so eloquently recited, would I be correct to assume you are indeed 'a bug of letters'?"

"You might assume that, if you wish. I am quite learned and teach at Lady Bug College at Yonder Bog."

I teach Creative Writing and English to lady bugs, and to all who are interested in learning. Three things you need to know about me. I am educated, I am pond-smart, and I'm over here. It's apparent that you can't see because you've been trying to focus on me and my whereabouts ever since I spoke to you. Why the tears and what's the problem?"

"I've misplaced my contact lenses and I can't see a thing. They're around here somewhere, but my eyesight is so bad that I couldn't see a stork if it was sitting next to me and you know how frogs hate and fear storks."

"I also told you that I am pond-smart. And being pond-smart,

I know that if you could see, my lifespan would be severely shortened. You would eat me, not talk to me. That's what frogs do—eat bugs."

"I would never do that," Big Bob swore. "On my saintly mother's memory, I would never do that to someone who would be willing to help me. Would you please be kind enough to help me, Tiny Bug?"

"Do you promise not to eat me?" Tiny Bug asked Big Bob

"Oh, I promise by everything precious to me, I promise, I promise, I promise not to eat you."

"Well I don't know what contact lenses are, or what they look like, but there's something strange lying behind you on the ground, next to the rock, at your right leg."

Big Bob was so excited. He started feeling everywhere, but in the wrong places.

"Do you know your right from your left?" Tiny Bug asked as Big Bob groped everywhere but in the right spot. "The other side, the other side," Tiny Bug said impatiently.

Trying the other side, Big Bob found the lenses immediately. He rinsed them off in the pond water and put them in.

"Oh thank you," he said excitedly. Big Bob was looking around everywhere and finally spied his new found friend and helper. "Oh, there you are. You are tiny, even for a lady bug."

"That's why they call me Tiny Bug. Well, glad to be able to help you. I must be going now."

Tiny Bug started to lift off and fly away, but it never happened. Big Bob had a vicious hunger pain and instinctively zapped Tiny Bug.

"Promises, promises," Big Bob said out loud as he savored the tiny morsel previously known as Tiny Bug. "How gullible can a bug be? I can't imagine anyone would believe that line about promising on their saintly mother's memory."

"I did," came a voice from the edge of the pond. "I did."

Big Bob whirled around and was eyeball to eyeball with a giant stork.

"Promises, promises," said the stork as he savored the morsel that was previously known as Big Bob.

It's truly amazing what a day can hold down at the pond. Bethy Wethy and Tony Turtle will have more to eat. A stork is now the new ruler of Lily Pad, and Lady Bug College at Yonder Bog is in the process of hiring a new teacher for Creative Writing and English.

HOW HIGH

My wife and I walk a lot at Meek's Park in Blairsville, GA. Thanks to Union County for such an excellent venue for exercise and family fun. The other day, while walking at the park, I made the comment to my wife of 45 years that men always have to do what their wives tell them to do.

My wife responded, "That's absurd and absolutely not true."

"Is too," I said. "If a wife says "jump," and her husband hears her, he will only have one question."

"I'm almost afraid to ask," my wife said, "and what would that question be?"

"HOW HIGH," was my reply.

"That's not true and you know it," she said in reply to my "HOW HIGH" answer.

It was a beautiful day and lots of people were walking. "Let's do a survey," I suggested. Two men were walking towards us on the track.

"Oh no, you're not," she responded, "they'll think you're crazy."

"Just for fun," I said as the two men approached us. "Excuse me," I said, "Could I ask you a question?"

The two men stopped and my wife said, "Don't pay him any attention."

I told them that I was doing a survey to settle a dispute

between us and had a question to ask married men or men who had been married. It was a good natured type of conversation and they were happy to co-operate with my survey. My wife rolled her eyes in disbelief.

"What is the question," one of the men asked.

"The question is this," I replied. "If your wife said the word "JUMP", what would your response be?"

You would have thought we had rehearsed this question and answer session for hours before hand. Without missing a beat and in perfect unison came their answer, "HOW HIGH?" We all had a good laugh and the older gentleman, who had told us that he would be 81 in August, gave me some more good advice for a long and healthy marriage. He informed me that there were also two other words I needed to remember and always be ready to use at a moment's notice.

"Do you know what those two words are?" he asked. It was my turn to answer a survey question and I said, "Tell me those magic words of wisdom."

He went on to say that if I ever had a disagreement with my wife, and if I knew that she was one-hundred-percent wrong, I should always respond in those situations with these two words, "Yes, dear."

We had another good laugh, and as we parted ways, my wife accused me of holding up cue cards with the answer "HOW HIGH" written on them.

Two women were approaching and my wife wanted to reverse the survey and ask them the same question. It was fine with me because it had turned into a fun sort of way to meet and talk with neighbors.

My wife stopped them and told them she needed their help. She explained that I had been asking men a question and had gotten an answer that she disagreed with. She asked if they would mind answering a question and they said, "Sure, go ahead."

"Here is the question," my wife said. "If your husband told you to "JUMP", what would your response be to him. One of the women just didn't get it, but the other one did and her response was not what my wife wanted to hear. "I wouldn't do anything," she replied, "I would ignore him."

The next survey contestant was another man. After explaining the survey and posing the question, we got the same response—"HOW HIGH?" Again, we laughed and walked on.

Two women were our next survey participants and it was great. After an explanation and a plea for help, my wife posed the question. The answers were great for me. The first woman said, "I wouldn't respond at all to that." The second woman said, "I never pay him any attention. When he tells me to do something, it goes in one ear and out the other." Not exactly the answers my wife was looking for.

This turned into a lot of fun and one of the best laps we ever walked in the park. One more man was approaching and he turned out to have the best answer of all for the "men's survey team." I explained to him that we were having a disagreement on an answer to something and asked if he would like to participate in our dilemma. I asked the question, "If your wife looked at you and said jump, what would your response be to her?"

"I would just start jumping," he said.

"That wasn't the exact answer I was looking for," I told him. "The answer I was looking for was "How High?"

"Oh no," the man responded. "When you have been married as long as I have you don't ask questions, you just jump."

I think we burned up more calories laughing that day than we did walking. Remembering the advice that the gentleman gave me earlier, I responded with a "yes, dear" when my wife informed me that my little survey was over.

WILLIAM AND JAMES—THE STORY OF TWO FLIES

William and James were best friends. They grew up together, and when William decided to move away, James went with him. They were actually cousins. William's mother was Bradley's sister, and Bradley was the father of James. The fact that they were cousins is not nearly as important as the fact that they were flies. But they were not your ordinary variety of houseflies. This family considered themselves to be restaurant flies.

William's father was called Big Al. Some family members suspected that there was a little horse somewhere in the genes. No one would dare say that in public, but Al was about twice as large as the other restaurant flies. He was also considered one of the smartest flies in the family. Every fly, finding himself in a dilemma, would ultimately end up asking Big Al for advice.

Big Al was very proud of William. He listened to his father's advice and tried to emulate his Dad as much as he could. Big Al would say, "That's my boy. He'll go far and do well."

Well, going far was on William's mind. He wanted to travel and see more of the world than just the local family diner where they lived. The diner was open six days a week but was closed on Sunday. Sundays were not good. All of the food was put away, the trash taken outside, and no customers came in to eat. This meant that Big Al and his family had to gorge themselves on Saturday to hold them over until the restaurant reopened on Monday.

Big Al gave William advice about what to look for and how to go about what to look for and how to go about selecting his new restaurant home. He shared with his son information that a very reputable fly had told him. "Restaurants with yellow signs are open seven days a week and twenty-four hours a day." That would be like paradise for a restaurant fly, allowing him to eat anytime he pleased.

Big Al gave William only one warning. Don't settle in a restaurant that doesn't speak English. He told William a very sad story. Their second cousin, Blow, had been killed in a restaurant where the cook did not speak English. It was a Mexican restaurant, and Spanish was their primary way of communicating. The cook told a waitress to get him the fly swatter, but he said it in Spanish. Blow didn't understand Spanish, and the cook killed him on the side of the grill.

Big Al was glad that his sister's kid, James, was going with William. Together, they could watch each other's back and as always, there is safety in numbers. William and James, armed with the info Big Al had given them, prepared to start out on their odyssey. This is their story, so I will let them take over from here.

"I'm ready," William told his family. "Are you ready, James?"

"As ready as I will ever be," James responded.

They had worked their way to the front of the restaurant and had landed on an unoccupied table near the door. The entire family had come into the dining area and they were scattered throughout the restaurant, out of harm's way, harm being the fly swatter.

"All right, James, when the next customer opens the door to come in, we're out of here."

'I'm ready," James replied.

The restaurant patrons could not hear it, but the entire family was rubbing their back legs together in a form of goodbye to this pair of adventurers. James and William returned the goodbye.

The door opened and they were gone. Big Al was very sad, but came around quickly, knowing that his son would do well. Once they were settled, William had promised to come back and tell them where he was living. Big Al had promised to visit as soon as he knew their address.

"Look out," William yelled at James. James almost flew into a truck that was coming into the restaurant parking lot.

"That was a close one," James said. They weren't used to being outside of the restaurant. Trucks and cars might prove to be more dangerous than a fly swatter.

"Remember," William told James, "to help me watch for a restaurant with a yellow sign. Hopefully, it will be easy to spot and close by as well."

"For sure," said James, "my wings are already getting tired."

Restaurant flies don't have a lot of stamina. Flying from storeroom to the dining area or from table to table doesn't require a lot of stamina. They seldom have to fly more than a few feet, and they never have to fly fast or get in a hurry. Unless, of course, someone is after them with a fly swatter. A few blocks to William and James would seem like a cross-country trek.

William saw a partially eaten sandwich that someone had thrown down on the ground. He did a 180 and James was right on his tail.

"Good eyes," James complimented William. "I could use something to eat about now. This traveling does make one hungry."

They settled down on the paper the sandwich had been wrapped in and had a feast.

"This isn't half bad," William commented. "It would be better if it was warm, but traveling flies can't be choosy. As soon as we find that restaurant with the yellow sign and get moved in and settled, we will have all the good, warm food that we want."

"For sure," James replied, "and I'm so looking forward to having our families come and visit us at our place. Won't that be nice?" James asked William.

"Absolutely," William responded. "Our folks will be so proud, and I wouldn't mind if they actually moved in with us. If Dad's source is correct and the restaurant with the yellow sign stays open seven days a week, and twenty-four hours a day, there would be plenty of food and no long Sundays without a meal. I know that home is a great place, but those Sundays without any food were tough. Mom and Dad and your folks as well need to be able to eat every day."

"I wouldn't mind either," James said in response to William's comment about the family moving in. "And besides, I hope we can do things a little differently than our parents. It was real easy to time the door this morning and fly out as the restaurant customers walked in. It would be just as easy to get back in by sitting outside the door and flying in as the customers walked in to have their meal."

"So, what are you saying?" William asked James.

"I'm saying, or suggesting, that we don't have to stay in the restaurant all of the time. We could fly out every once in a while, and maybe eat somewhere like this. It would be a change of scenery, and I think it would do us good to get outside in the fresh air."

"You know," William said, "I like your idea about being mobile. It would be nice to get out, see a little bit of the neighborhood and find some different types of food. You never know what might be next door. And if we never go out, we'll never know."

"Truer words were never spoken," James said.

"Whatever are you talking about?" William asked.

"Look across the street," James replied.

"Well, I'll be a June bug," William said. "It was just across the street. We never saw it because no one ever ventured outside of the diner. It was there all the time, and to think of all the Sundays we sat in that diner, hungry, and the yellow sign restaurant was just next door."

"That proves the value of traveling," James said, "you'll never know what's out there until you get out and take a look."

As James and William finished their meal, it was truly amazing for them to look at their old home and to look on the corner, just across the street, at their new home.

"Had enough to eat," William asked James as a courtesy before taking flight to the yellow signed restaurant.

"Sure enough," James responded. "I have a bite or two stashed under my wing for an emergency, just in case we have trouble getting inside our new home with the yellow sign."

"We won't have any trouble getting in," William stated confidently. "Boy, will Dad ever be surprised to find out that the restaurant with the yellow sign was just next door and we could have moved over there anytime. Sometimes, the younger flies outsmart the older flies."

William and James had a big laugh and felt good about their find. Big Al had given them great advice and had the utmost confidence that his son would do well in life. The one thing that Big Al didn't teach William was how to read. That's because flies don't read; neither house flies nor restaurant flies.

They lifted off the sandwich paper with ease and flew with confidence toward their new home. They landed outside and waited for the next customer to come up and go in so that they could gain access to the restaurant with the yellow sign, the one that stayed open seven days a week, twenty-four hours a day.

It is a shame that they couldn't read. The yellow sign said, "Poncho's Mexican Restaurant." It was also a shame that they could not see in the kitchen. The cook, who only spoke Spanish, had two fly swatters. A customer came up to the door, opened it, and all three went in.

POSSUMS OF HEAVEN

There's no doubt they're ugly and when confronted, they'll snarl and hiss. They move slowly, seemingly unafraid of danger and are most often seen lying dead in the road. The lowly possum, handiwork of the Almighty, was created specifically to be His eyes and ears at night. Operating under the cover of darkness, they witness the evil things men and women do when they think no one is watching. But the possums see it all. And they report back to Gabriel, who, you guessed it, forwards the report to the Almighty.

In the beginning, they were beautiful creations, as cute and cuddly as bunny rabbits. Over time, the vile, despicable, and deplorable things they had to witness changed their outward appearance to what we see them as today.

Being in the service of the Lord, they are glory bound. At the end of their life, they'll be changed in the twinkling of an eye back into a thing of beauty. When you see a dead possum lying in the roadway, rejoice. I say again, rejoice. That possum is no longer having to snarl and hiss at the wickedness witnessed on earth, and it is no longer ugly. Having died in the service of the Lord, they are now walking the streets of Glory.

God is good, His mercy is everlasting, and His creations are beautiful.

LEGEND OF RAOUL

Chicken wasn't always a term that referred to cowardice. In 1863, the word chicken struck fear in the hearts of men; if not all men, at least the men who worked on Booger Holler Plantation.

It was a time when families were divided, brothers were killing brothers, and chaos was the order of the day. Booger Holler Plantation would be the birthplace of the modern term we know as "chicken", referring to someone who is scared to death, spineless, and basically a mass of quivering cowardice. When someone yelled "chicken" on the Booger Holler Plantation, pandemonium would become the order of the moment. Grown men would faint and lie in a comatose state until the crisis had passed. Hence, the word "chicken" came into our vernacular.

Things had not always been this way on the plantation. As a matter of fact, chicken had originally been a very joyful word and conjured up images of wonderful meals to be enjoyed by everyone. Fried chicken, baked chicken, roasted chicken, barbeque chicken, stir-fry chicken, chicken for lunch, and chicken for dinner. The chicken sandwich would come later. That's another story.

This tragic story of the demise of Booger Holler Plantation began innocently enough. Mr. Johnson, the owner of the plantation, bought a large number of chickens from a friend who had imported them from Sweden. They were touted as being far superior in hardiness and in egg production. This Swedish chicken was supposed to be the most scrumptious chicken one could put in their mouth and even came with a recipe for Swedish chicken casserole. The fly in this ointment was Raoul.

Raoul was no ordinary rooster. His Swedish owner, Gustaf, loved all kinds of barnyard creatures and especially hens and roosters. He would read to them, sing to them, and let them come and go as they pleased. He enjoyed the eggs but never plucked a single feather from one of his beloved friends. As he would sing, they would often join in and cluck and scratch to the beat of the song.

Gustaf recognized that Raoul had far greater intelligence than any fowl he had ever encountered. He was getting up in years and wanted to make sure Raoul had every opportunity to succeed in life. America was where the future seemed to lie, even for a rooster. With great sadness, he sent Raoul and one hundred of his finest hens to a new beginning. That new beginning would be on Booger Holler Plantation.

On the plantation, chickens were free to go and come as they pleased. The term free-range would be applied later. Raoul noticed the number of his Swedish hen-friends was declining. Whenever one or more of the hens was caught and placed in a coop, they disappeared and were never seen again. This troubled Raoul greatly.

What would trouble him more was the introduction of a

younger, more virile, new rooster. Raoul was no dummy. He watched the new rooster strut his stuff. Every morning, the new rooster would try and out-crow Raoul.

"No one needs two wake-up calls," Raoul thought to himself.

One morning Raoul was in hot pursuit of a June bug that had been buzzing the horse paddock. Catching a quick glimpse of a shadow, Raoul realized someone was stalking him. Stalking escalated into full-blown capture mode, and Raoul just barely escaped with all of his feathers intact.

Having been Swedish-born smart, Raoul selected the safety of the woods to contemplate the situation at hand. Hen-friends, chased and caught, were never seen again. He surmised that if his attacker had captured him, he would have been put in the coop also and would have disappeared from the landscape.

He spent his evenings and nights perched in trees for safety. There he formulated his plan. All of the Swedish hens were his friends and perhaps a little more than just friends. With that thought, Raoul blushed.

A band of free-range chickens was about to be assembled from the Booger Holler barnyard. He would take them, one or two at a time, and get them to a safe zone in the woods. The plan sounded simple, but nothing is as simple as it sounds.

Raoul was nearly captured during several daytime raids. He had rescued only twenty-one of his hen-friends and had come to realize the Booger Holler contingent of workers was not about to surrender without a fight. He couldn't take it to another level, but he could take it to a different level.

Chickens are supposed to sleep at night. Raoul would become a guerrilla rooster and strike in the dark. This was risky business for Raoul because his natural predators hunted at night. There were nineteen more original Swedish hen-friends in harm's way, and he meant to bring them out to safety.

It was summertime and Booger Holler Plantation had not yet installed air conditioning. Gaining entrance to the house would be easy. Night after night, Raoul would rescue one or two hens and get them to the safe zone. He would then return, enter the house, and inflict damage and leave casualties in his wake.

No one in the house was safe. He would fly up on their beds, scratch and peck and then would disappear. During one of the attacks, someone saw a rooster. Raoul had been gone for a while, so the next morning, the new rooster paid the ultimate price. The attacks continued until Raoul had rescued all of his hen-friends.

A boldness was now coursing through Raoul's veins. His hen-friends were safe. There was an abundance of food for the scratching and plenty of trees for nighttime safety. All of Booger Holler's residents were now sleeping in one room. They kept the door and windows closed and almost suffocated from the heat. They were like walking zombies from lack of sleep and therefore easy daytime targets.

The hen-friends tried to dissuade Raoul from going back on daytime raids. He had already achieved hero status in their eyes. Raoul was the stuff legends are made of. He had developed a swagger that made his hen-friends swoon, and he assured them he would make only a few more trips.

"The residents of Booger Holler Plantation need to remember Raoul is out here and is afraid of nothing," he told his admirers.

Raoul knew where to attack in order to do the most damage. He knew who would be his target and he planned the point of attack, literally. Mr. Johnson, the plantation owner, was the mark. The privy out back was the place of attack. And the point of attack, well, you figure that one out for yourself. Let's just say the door of the privy was knocked completely from its hinges, and the most embarrassing run for the house ever witnessed took place.

Raoul returned to his hen-friends, and over time they multiplied and filled the surrounding woods with free-range chickens. But the legend was born and the legend lives today.

Today, the world's insatiable taste for chicken is bigger than any one Raoul. But the legend still lives. In crowded chicken houses the world over, Raoul is remembered. The situations today are far worse than those of the Booger Holler Plantation.

As many as forty-thousand chickens are crowded into one chicken house. Food and water are available 24/7. The lifespan is thirty-five to sixty days. They are caught by hand at night and placed in cages much like the coops of Raoul's day.

Their first ride was to the chicken house as baby chicks, and their last ride is to the processing plant. They have lived a very short life, the maximum being sixty days. If you ever see a poultry truck on the way to the processing plant, take a close look at the poor, bewildered chickens. Most have their eyes closed tightly to keep out the fifty to sixty-five mph winds generated on the highway. Feathers fly from the crates as they make their final trip. With eyes closed, they remember the legend. In their minds they feel fear, but in their hearts they have hope—Raoul will come in time. Raoul will save them.

PEW JUMPING

It was Communion Sunday. Brother Alan was having lower back problems accompanied by spasms that sometimes made him holler out in pain. He told his wife, Pam, that he wasn't going to church because he was afraid that when he knelt at the altar after partaking in communion, he might have one of those spasms, and he didn't want to disrupt the service by crying out in pain. Sister Pam got out the Tylenol and informed Brother Alan he would be going to church. "You'll be fine," she told her husband.

Brother Bill and his wife Anne also attended the same church and had been members there for about a year. They had formerly been members of a local Pentecostal Church, and in his day, Brother Bill had quite a reputation for being a pew jumper. They changed their membership from the Pentecostal Church to the United Methodist Church after an unfortunate event occurred, creating an embarrassing situation.

You see, one Sunday morning in the Pentecostal Church, when Brother Bill got caught up in the spirit, he began his usual spirit-filled activity of running across the backs of the pews. He was quite proficient in that area.

Sister Alice was either slain in the spirit or napping in the pew. No one knows for sure which one it was, but she was sprawled out on one of the pews near the back of the church. Brother Bill was going flat-out and was about to jump the pew when she unexpectedly sat up.

Brother Bill, who had never had to stop in mid-air before, did. He took Sister Alice out, much like a pass rusher takes out a quarterback. Her glasses were broken and her wig landed four rows behind her. When she came to, it wasn't an unknown tongue she spoke in. It was pretty much the tongue you might hear in a bar where a drunken brawl was taking place.

Brother Bill was transported to the hospital. That Sunday, he learned a valuable lesson. If one is going to stop in mid-air while going flat-out across the backs of the pews, one had truly better be in the Spirit. The ER doctor told him he would be fine in a few weeks. He had a broken collarbone, four broken ribs and a severely sprained ankle. The ER doctor, an unbeliever, told Brother Bill the backs of the pews should be used to lean against while sitting, not falling against with one's collarbone and rib cage. The emergency room visit was anything but an opportunity for Brother Bill to witness. It only further enhanced the position of the doctor.

Brother Bill was so embarrassed by this incident he couldn't face his former church members. He bought new glasses for Sister Alice and had her wig redone. Feeling like remaining a member of the Pentecostal Church was not an option, Brother Bill and his wife Anne moved their membership to the same United Methodist Church, that Brother Alan and his wife Pam attended.

There would be no pew jumping at the United Methodist Church. They had a very orderly and reverent service. It was a spirit-filled church, without the gym-like workout sessions Brother Bill had enjoyed for so many years. The new church had a guaranteed service time of one hour. On Sunday mornings, members of the congregation were always the first to arrive at the local restaurants for lunch. Brother Alan liked that. Brother Bill did not.

The people at the United Methodist Church were very friendly and Brother Bill and Sister Anne made lots of new friends. But once a pew jumper, always a pew jumper. During the services, Brother Bill would sometimes feel the spirit move, but it quickly stopped moving because his wife Anne would dig her long fingernails into his leg. This would immediately de-pentecostalize him.

While liking his new church, he longed for his old church and the spirit-filled services he had participated in. In his pew jumping days, Brother Bill was in excellent physical shape. Now he was overweight, and the least bit of physical activity left him short of breath. He secretly blamed this on the type of services his new United Methodist Church conducted.

So, Brother Bill decided that what his new church needed was what his old church had, and he began praying for the orderly, reverent services to be replaced by spirit-filled services like he had experienced in his old church. He adopted a line from the movie, *Angels in the Outfield*, where the little boy kept saying, 'It could happen.'"

On this particular Sunday morning, Sister Pam made Brother Alan go to church, bad back and all. He took the Tylenol like his wife prescribed and when the communion service started, he went to the altar to participate.

Brother Bill had bowed his head and was praying for a stirring of the Spirit like he used to experience in his old church. When Brother Alan tried to kneel down to take Communion, a back spasm grabbed him, and he let out a blood-curdling scream from the pain the Tylenol wasn't handling. Brother Bill took this as a sign his prayers had been answered. Immediately, he jumped to his feet and started running the aisles. Well, running might be a stretch, because he still had a limp from his last pew jumping experience. His wife Anne also jumped to her feet. She wasn't in the spirit, she was simply trying to catch her husband before he hurt somebody else. She was having flashbacks of Sister Alice's wig flying through the air. Because of the limp, Anne was able to collar her husband before he could climb up on the back of the pews. It was clear to the whole congregation who was the boss in that family when Sister Anne pointed to the door and marched Brother Bill out to the parking lot and into their car. That was the last time they ever attended services there.

From time to time, while waiting to be seated at one of their favorite restaurants, someone from the United Methodist Church would recall the day when Anne tackled her husband in the center aisle near the altar. And someone would bring up the fact that no one ever figured out why Brother Bill was trying to climb up on the back of the pew. Then someone else would remember that it was the same service where Brother Alan had the back spasm and screamed so loudly while trying to kneel to take communion.

By this time, the subject would usually change, as the waitress brought their beverages and members began to place their lunch orders. And on that particular Sunday, like any other, the United Methodist Church members were the first to arrive at the restaurant, because, after all, their services are orderly, reverent, and guaranteed to be over in an hour.

Section 2

IT'S A GRAND OLD FLAG

It's a great country and a grand old flag. Thank God, extremists on the left, and on the right, can get permits for rallies. Thank God, Democrats and Republicans, Liberals and Conservatives, and Progressives and Libertarians can agree to disagree. It's a great country and a grand old flag.

Thank God anyone can picket or protest anything or any cause, with only one requirement—that it be peaceful in nature. It's a great country and a grand old flag. Try taking a knee in North Korea, Syria, or Iran. Let us know how that works out for you. It's a great country and a grand old flag.

I pledge allegiance to the flag of the United States of America and to the Republic for which it stands, one nation, under God, indivisible, with liberty and justice for all. It's a great country and a grand old flag.

COUNT YOUR BLESSINGS

My intention was to have breakfast at a local café—eggs, bacon and toast, my usual. The main course served that morning was spiritual food, not the usual fare in a café. I was nursing some aches and pains with the usual accompanying pity party and feeling a little sorry for myself. God always has such a wonderful way of getting our attention. Sometimes it's subtle, and other times His wisdom and love will explode on the scene and overwhelm you. That morning, I would get both.

An older gentleman, eating alone, got up from his table and started to leave. For no apparent reason, he turned to me and said, "The brothers, Arthritis and Bursitis, are at it again, but it's such a beautiful day, I'm not going to let them get the best of me." He smiled, and with great difficulty, headed to the cashier.

I couldn't help but notice erratic behavior in the booth across from me. It didn't take long to figure out the problem. A man had brought his wife out for breakfast and she had Alzheimer's. She kept getting up and announcing it was time to go home. Her husband would lovingly stand up, get her to sit back down, and encourage her to eat her breakfast. Before he could take two bites, she would stand up again and he would patiently repeat the process.

God had my attention, and I felt so bad about my insignificant problems. And then for good measure, he had a man with only one arm stop by for breakfast. I understood the lesson God was teaching me and immediately recalled one of my grandmother's favorite hymns, *Count Your Blessings.*

The words flowed through my mind like healing waters; "Count your blessings, name them one by one. Count your many blessings see what God hath done."

FIRST MIRACLE

It had been a long week—all weeks are long when a chemo treatment is involved. Marie, my wife of 24 years, had just received her fifth treatment. She had lost all of her beautiful hair and was very nauseous most of the time. She ate very little and drank even less. Pancreatic cancer isn't kind to anyone, and she had been diagnosed as stage 4.

There's not a good time to have any kind of cancer, but Christmas might be one of the worst seasons for chemo treatments. She had tried to help decorate the house and wanted to use snowmen as the theme for this year. Any effort at all left her exhausted. She had insisted I put up the Nativity scene in the front of our home. It was beautiful and everyone enjoyed riding by at night and seeing the Wise Men, shepherds, sheep, and of course, Mary, Joseph, and the baby Jesus.

It was bedtime and I was exhausted. Marie was already in bed asleep. I cut all of the Christmas lights off, including the spotlight on the Nativity scene. I laid down next to her, gently took her hand and prayed for healing. Many friends at church and family members were also holding her up in prayer, pleading for a miracle.

I was awakened by an unfamiliar sound, rolled over and looked at the clock. It was 3 AM. Listening, and not hearing the sound again, I turned over to go back to sleep. Then I heard it again. It sounded like a sheep bleating. That couldn't be, because there were no sheep, or any other animals besides dogs and cats in our neighborhood. I heard it a third time and got out of bed to investigate.

I went out on our back deck, listened and didn't hear anything. As I started through the house toward the front door, I saw a light in the vicinity of the Nativity scene. I thought for a second, but knew I had turned the spotlight off. Opening the front door and stepping out onto the porch, I had the shock of my life. The figures in the manger scene were approximately three to four feet tall. The sheep, obviously, smaller still. What I saw was a six foot Joseph, smiling and extending his hand in my direction. The three kings and the angel were also turned facing me. I must be losing my mind, I thought. It only got worse from there. Mary stood and took a few steps in my direction. Joseph immediately went to her side to steady her. The baby Jesus was asleep in the manger.

"Go and get Marie," Mary said softly, "and bring her to the manger.

As crazy as this dream seemed to be, I still had some sense of reality and said, "Marie is very sick and can't come outside."

"Go and get Marie," she said again, not with authority, but with love and concern.

They were all watching me to see what I would do. I knew I

was in some kind of dream world or perhaps a nightmare, but turned and went back inside the house. I didn't close the door. I walked into our bedroom, but had no intention of waking Marie and introducing her to my dream, or whatever it was. I heard steps and turned to see Mary walking up to the bed. Marie awakened instantly, but didn't seem to see Mary.

"What is it, John?" she asked.

I wasn't sure what was happening, but I knew Mary was standing right next to me, and I also knew that was impossible. Mary, or the representation of Mary, was molded plastic and made to sit by the manger, three feet tall at best, not five plus feet tall when standing at my side. Marie managed to sit up on the side of the bed.

"What is it, John?" she asked a second time.

"Here goes nothing," I said to myself. "Honey, how would you like to go outside to see the Nativity scene? It's beautiful at night. It's not too chilly and we could take a blanket, cover up and sit in the swing for a few minutes. What do you think, honey?"

"Get my housecoat and help me up. There's a blanket on the couch. It's large enough to cover both of us. Something different might be better than lying in bed all the time. When we turned to head to the front door, Mary was not there. Maybe she was never there—maybe it was a hallucination.

As we slowly started up the hallway toward the front door, I heard the sheep bleating again.

"What was that?" Marie asked.

I felt faint and wasn't sure who was helping who at this point. The light, or glow, was still visible as we approached the doorway. Stepping onto the porch, I heard Marie take a deep breath and falter a little as we took a couple of more steps.

Again, everyone had turned to look at us. Two of the kings bowed at the waist, and the third bowed his head toward Marie. Mary stood, and took a few steps from the manger. She smiled at Marie and motioned for her to come to her. Marie smiled back and I felt her trying to take a step toward Mary. "This isn't happening," I said aloud. Marie squeezed my arm, further blowing my mind. Apparently, I wasn't the only one lost in this delusion. Marie seemed at peace with what she was looking at.

Joseph met us at the step and extended his hand to my Marie. Taking his hand, she looked up at me and smiled, and then left me standing on the step. I followed behind the two of them, like a lost puzzle piece. Joseph, or the replica of Joseph, I wasn't sure at this point, took Marie to Mary.

Mary took Marie's hand and helped her to sit down on some hay someone had fashioned into a makeshift seat. Baby Jesus woke up and was looking at his mother and my wife.

"Marie," Mary asked, "would you like to hold my newborn son?"

Marie smiled and held out her arms, answering Mary's question with the gesture. Mary picked the baby up and placed Him in Marie's arms. She was all smiles as the baby kicked and squirmed in her lap.

As she coddled baby Jesus, I became acutely aware of where we both were. My spirit made me aware that we were smack dab in the middle of a miracle in progress. I looked again at my wife. Her hair was growing right before my eyes. My eyes watered and tears ran down my face. Joseph walked over and put his arm around my shoulders. Mary sat and smiled as baby Jesus performed His first miracle, one that wasn't recorded anywhere. I could see the old Marie as strength once again filled her body. I slipped to the ground, offering praise to God for what I knew was a special Christmas gift to us.

A few minutes passed and Mary held out her arms and Marie returned the child to her. "Tell no one what has happened here tonight," Mary told Marie. Hearing what she said, we both nodded and agreed to keeping the secret. Smiling, Marie stood, walked over to where I was kneeling, and helped me to my feet. We both turned and looked at all the characters gathered in our front yard. They all smiled a knowing smile. A sheep bleated again, and I told Marie it was time to go back inside. As we entered the house, we both turned again for a last look. Everything was back to normal. The characters were again small and lifeless.

Baby Jesus was back in the manger and his mother was again at His side.

The doctor's made a pronouncement no physician could write a prescription for. A miracle had taken place and they had no explanation. We told them nothing. As Jesus went around performing miracles, he would tell the recipients to tell no one. Mary had told us the same thing. However, when you come face to face with the Son of God, it's hard not to shout and praise His name and tell everyone what He had done for you.

Twenty years have passed and she is still cancer free. We have kept our promise—sort of. My name isn't John and my wife's name isn't Marie, but His name is Wonderful, Counselor, Mighty God, Everlasting Father, Prince of Peace.

LOVE THY NEIGHBOR

The Hills cry out and the Stars look down with sadness as mankind struggles with the basic directive of creation. A directive so simple, the Sun and Moon, in conversation, ask how could man fail to understand the instruction. The Sky, joining in the discussion, suggests the directive was too simple.

The Wind, traveling far and wide, entered the conversation, telling a story she had just witnessed in the city. Rush hour traffic had come to a standstill. It was bitter cold as she whipped through the city. A homeless man had settled in under a bridge next to the freeway. He had covered up with newspapers, rags, and an old coat. He was hungry, cold, and sick.

With the traffic at, or near a standstill, drivers looked over at the concrete abutment and most of them determined from inside their warm cars that the homeless man was there because of the choices he had made in life. What the Wind saw and the drivers did not see, was the Angel standing next to the homeless man. Nor did they hear the Angel tell the Wind that the people's hearts were colder than the freezing temperatures outside their cars. That evening the Angel had come as an escort. The homeless man would be hungry, cold, and sick for a little while longer.

At that moment, Rainbow joined the conversation. Rainbow believed in people, and she contended that one day the people would remember the Creator's simple directive: Love Thy Neighbor.

WHERE'S PAPA?

There are seven in all—seven beautiful grandchildren. But only one is left—six have been taken from me. College has two of them. The abyss, also known as the teen-age years, has two of them, and iPads, swim lessons, dance lessons, and scouts hold the other two hostage. When we visit, only one wakes up asking, "Where's Papa?"

She holds my finger when I walk her to the playground, unafraid and trusting. Her Papa is with her, and he knows stuff. Riding in her stroller, she never considers the age of her Papa, as he labors to get up the steep hillsides.

"Where's Papa?"

"He's walking me to the playground or taking me for a ride in my stroller."

To some, the white hair and advanced years signal diminished capacity. But not to her; our relationship is the last bastion of hope bridging the generations.

"Where's Papa?" is a beautiful question asked by my three-year old granddaughter.

SUNDAY SNOW

On most Sunday mornings, immediately following church, a number of us will go to an area restaurant for lunch. There is a standing joke that our church has the best minister in town because he has a watch and an appetite that matches ours. We are almost always out of the service and on our way to a predetermined restaurant by 12:00 noon on the dot. We have usually been seated and have placed our orders before the other churches start having reps show up. We joke about being faster on the draw than our Christian friends, but it's in jest, and we do it in a good-natured manner.

This Sunday, it would be different. We should have gone to the grocery store on Saturday, but that's another story. We didn't. This morning, we awoke with several inches of fresh snow, and predictions of dropping temperatures and ice coming in on Monday.

There would be no problem getting to church, but after church we needed to go directly to the grocery store to stock up. In the small mountain community where we live, you can never tell how long winter storms will last. Sunday brunch with our friends would have to take the back burner. The choice was between eating today with our church friends, or stocking up and eating all next week. My wife and I chose the latter.

Our area roads are well maintained by the highway department and crews had already spread a sufficient amount of salt and gravel. As expected, the grocery store parking lot was full. Apparently, a lot of people were out of a lot of things. I thought to myself, "The restaurants will not be crowded this morning."

I let my wife out at the entrance, and as I started to look for a parking space, I got lucky. A customer was backing out, and I was able to park right at the front door. I usually sit in the car and wait while she does the shopping.

This morning, Mother Nature had done well. She had covered the parking lot with the whitest blanket of snow imaginable. All the litter, cigarette butts and oil spots, usually associated with parking lots, was gone. The world had been cleansed, or at least covered well.

We have a large contingency of retirees in our area, and they were out in force. Bag boys, out to retrieve the shopping carts, threw snowballs at each other. One senior citizen joined in and was throwing snowballs with the bag boys. It was nice to see them cut her some slack. They could have buried her, but they didn't.

The snow, in addition to giving a fresh appearance to the parking lot, also seemed to put a little spring in the steps of the shoppers. Though it was only 26 degrees, smiles were displayed by almost everyone coming from and going into the store. One teenager, walking with his Mom, tried to catch snowflakes on his tongue. It looked amusing to see someone walking across a parking lot with his tongue stuck out as far as it would go.

I had an awesome parking place. I could see everything and everyone. It seemed, at least in the parking lot, that a nice blanket of fresh snow had made everything right in the world again. On a normal snow-free day, shoppers come and go, without expression, very few exhibiting smiles or any signs of happiness. After all, I guess, it's just a grocery store. But the snow, this blanket of white, seemed to work magic, even in my own mind and heart.

It felt like a magical time until a certain family came out of the store—a man, a woman, and three small children. The woman was pushing the grocery cart, and there wasn't much in it. The children ranged in ages from six to perhaps ten years old. The woman looked tired and bedraggled. The man, bringing up the rear, stopped to light a cigarette and put the hood of his sweatshirt up over his ball cap. His clothes were worn and his tennis shoes looked very old. One shoe wasn't tied , and the strings trailed in the snow.

This was the only unhappiness I had witnessed in the snow-covered parking lot. The man and woman were clearly disconnected in spirit, and the children were caught somewhere in the middle of that relationship. Perhaps more than a blanket of snow was needed here.

I picked out what I thought was their vehicle before they got to it. An older model Ford pickup truck, very battered, sat next to the building; they hadn't bothered to park in a designated parking place. The woman placed the few groceries in the back seat area and got in behind the wheel. The man stood outside finishing his cigarette while the children played in the snow.

Hearing the pickup engine roar to life, I watched as smoke billowed from the tailpipe. Then I witnessed the miracle of the snow again. One of the boys stuck out his tongue and was trying to catch snowflakes. The other two children did the same thing, and laughter broke out as all three children danced around in the snow. All I had surmised to be missing in this family was quickly overpowered by the fresh falling snow and the magic it possessed for the children. But the snow was not magic for everyone. The children climbed into the back seat area of the truck. The man, as he was getting in front next to his wife, thumped his cigarette butt onto the fresh, fallen snow.

I looked over toward the entrance to the grocery store and saw my wife coming out with a cart full of groceries. Her grocery list had been long enough to allow me sufficient time to see the majesty of God in the snowfall, the happiness it brings to those who embrace it, and the sadness and heartache it cannot overcome.

MANTIS RELIGIOSA

People can pray in church and out of church. They can pray anywhere and anytime. But what makes a praying mantis pray? Perhaps a more perplexing question would be, what makes a praying mantis go to church to pray?

Such were my thoughts one Sunday morning. Sitting inside the church, I noticed a large praying mantis sitting on the window ledge looking inside at the congregation. At least he seemed to be looking inside; hard to know for sure. I found it difficult to listen to the sermon because I was preoccupied with this visitor, at my church, on the window ledge and next to my pew.

He seemed focused and moved very little. With his face pressed hard against the glass, I wondered if he was trying to hear the sermon our pastor was delivering. Can a praying mantis hear? Can they see, and if so, how well do they see? He seemed to be looking in the direction of the pulpit and was definitely paying more attention than me.

As the service was coming to a close, I had every intention of going outside to get a closer look at our visitor. The choir had a short chorus and the pastor gave the benediction.

When I opened my eyes and looked over at the window ledge, the praying mantis was gone. Outside, he was nowhere to be found.

At home, I looked up praying mantis on the internet and found out some interesting facts about *mantis religiosa*. Their front legs, held together on an angle, suggests they are praying. They definitely can see, having two large compound eyes and three other simple eyes between the large ones. The information found on the internet helped me figure out why this praying mantis had decided to visit my church. This mantis was a she, and had come to church because her conscience had gotten the best of her. The internet article said the female praying mantis often eats the male mantis after mating. I assumed this was the case and she had come to church, seeking absolution.

FORGIVENESS

There are two types of forgiveness; *ordinary* forgiveness and *divine* forgiveness.

Ordinary forgiveness is meted out often and covers the everyday happenings that require apologies. Most of the time ordinary forgiveness covers things that probably don't really matter and the "I'm sorry" offered is familiar to all of us. No one will suffer damage of any consequence and life will continue without interruption.

Divine forgiveness is required when the hurt is so deep and the pain is so great that considerable damage has been done. A simple "I'm sorry" will not suffice. The very soul of the injured party cries out for justice. Something has occurred that blots out happiness and reason, and destroys the spirit of the person who was wronged.

This type of forgiveness can only originate with the Divine. Jesus, crucified for our sins, set the example and taught us how to forgive the great and terrible wrongs that we sometimes suffer and endure at the hands of others. On the cross, Jesus said, "Father, forgive them, for they know not what they do" (Luke 23:34).

Let us always remember the example Jesus set for us. When something happens in our life and we cannot find forgiveness in our hearts, let us remember that Jesus can provide healing and help us to find forgiveness, even as He displayed it on the Cross.

—Ephesians 4:32

Be ye kind, one to another, forgiving one another, even as God for Christ's sake has forgiven you.

CHRISTMAS MEMORIES

It's Christmas time. My wife always remarks, "It has *snuck* up on us again." I like the word "snuck", but that's not the case. Shopping, decorating, shopping, writing Christmas cards, shopping, Christmas gatherings, and more shopping doesn't indicate to me Christmas snuck up on us. It's been bearing down on us like the Siberian Express.

The majority of my Christmas memories are happy ones. But with the passing of so many Christmas seasons, I find myself at the head of the table occupying a place recognizing my senior status. It's easy to see Christmases Past and to visualize my parents, along with so many other dear family members, gathered around the Christmas dinner table.

After dinner, we would gather around the tree for the opening of gifts. My Dad would pretend he didn't want anything, but we all knew that wasn't the truth. He was as excited as the grandchildren. Anticipation created a noise level that almost made hearing the names being called out for gifts nearly impossible to understand.

After Mom passed, my wife would put up a small artificial Christmas tree in Dad's home. She would insist that he go Christmas shopping with her for the grandkids. With reluctance, he would go. On Christmas morning, he would immediately take down the little tree and put it back in the closet where it would patiently wait until the next Christmas. He would drive up to our house and say proudly, "I've already taken my Christmas tree down." He thought that was so funny.

Each Christmas, I now put Dad's small tree up in our home. I place memorabilia around the tree, such as Mom and Dad's 50th Anniversary Card, the flour sifter that she used to make the best biscuits in the world, Dad's last wallet, and his keys. There is also a plastic duck Dad won in the second grade, and an address book of men he served with in World War II. For our family it's a good thing, remembering at Christmas time those who were so special in our lives.

The most special piece of the past for me is a pair of shoes that belonged to my father when he was a baby. They are now approximately ninety years old. A lot of Christmas seasons have snuck into the past since he wore them. On the bottom of one of the shoes is some red Georgia clay. I can't help but wonder what he was doing or where he was going on that particular day, so long ago.

Merry Christmas, Dad, we miss you!

STORM CLOUDS

Lord, this mountain looms larger than life and storm clouds are gathered all around us. But we remember Your promise, Lord—"Where two or more are gathered in Your name, You are in their midst" (Matthew 18:20).

Praying without ceasing, we lift our prayers to You. Lord, we believe You hear us, and we believe we will hear from Heaven.

We remember the woman with the issue of blood. We remember blind Bartimaeus and the daughter of Jairus. The things You did for those people, You will also do for us. We believe Lord, help our unbelief.

BLESSED

The early morning mountain air is crisp and clean. In the grocery store, my wife shops for food. In the grass, next to where I am parked, several sparrows do the same.

People entering the store represent young and old. Some with a spring in their step, and some with only a few springs left. Scripture comes to mind as I watch the people and sparrows. I started to tell the sparrows about the Scripture, but realized they already knew. In thinking about the sparrows, I thought about the hairs on my head. I smile at the fact God doesn't have to spend as much time as He used to, counting them. The sparrows are blessed, and so am I.

A GRANDMOTHER'S LEGACY

Indian Springs Holiness Campground was founded in 1890. There is a plaque on the grounds where five very devout men prayed, asking God's guidance in selecting a place to build the campground. The campground was founded on Wesleyan doctrine and a belief in entire sanctification as a second work of Grace. That is all I will give you of the camp history.

A special event would occur fifty-seven years later. On December 17, 1947, I was born. Indian Springs camp meeting is usually held during the first two weeks in August. My grandmother had two rooms in one of the annex buildings directly behind the tabernacle. My grandfather never went to camp meeting. My grandmother, accompanied by two of her grown daughters, never missed camp meeting. I attended my first camp meeting during the summer of 1948, and according to family stories, I was kept in a card board box in the annex.

There was a bathroom on each end of the porch and the rooms had open ceilings. I would attend camp meeting for the next sixteen years without missing a summer. My grandmother never missed either and always made sure I was there. She passed away when I was ten years old. She made me attend every service, including the early morning prayer services in the tabernacle. I usually went to services three times a day. I was privileged to hear some of the best preachers Asbury Theological Seminary ever produced. It was hot under the open tabernacle in August. Hotter still were the holiness messages that would shape my life.

When my grandmother passed away, my two aunts made sure her wishes were followed and continued to take me to camp meeting.

Clay Milby was the song leader for years. I played in the orchestra every summer, and can still hear in my mind a song we did every Sunday morning, "Some Glad Morning." It was one of my grandmother's favorites.

My wife and I had a cabin at the Nazarene Campground in Adrian, GA for a number of years. The Nazarene denomination also preached heart holiness and believed in entire sanctification as a definite, second work of grace. We raised our two children in churches that preached scriptural holiness. They attended many camp meetings, including Indian Springs, which is still going strong.

Our children and grandchildren have been influenced mightily by my grandmother. They are not perfect; none of us are. But God is at the center of their homes and lives, and I believe it all started with my grandmother humming "Some Glad Morning" to a baby boy in a cardboard box on the porch of Annex A at Indian Springs Holiness Camp Ground.

WHAT GOES AROUND, COMES AROUND

Across the restaurant, a father and son were having breakfast. Their resemblance was unmistakable. The father, if I had to guess, was thirty-five or so, and his son, around fourteen. I couldn't hear the conversation. They talked easily, but with passion. They smiled a lot and when the boy laughed, it was infectious and caused me to smile as well.

I assumed they were talking about something special to both of them—sports, fishing or the like. I wanted to go over and sit with them and enjoy this all too familiar memory once again. Actually, I wanted to roll back the hands of time, not permanently, just long enough to enjoy one more meal with my son, the way this father was doing. To talk sports, to laugh easily, and to revisit a special relationship that comes and goes all too quickly.

As I walked by their table, I strained to hear what they were talking about. I wanted to stop and tell them to enjoy this special time in their lives because it is so fleeting. My son, thirty-five years old lives a great distance from me. His son, my grandson, also has an infectious laugh. There is a good chance they are also having breakfast, talking easily and laughing often. What goes around, comes around.

FAMILY TRADITION

It was an evening to remember. My son and his nine-year-old son, my Dad and me; four generations at the same table, the day after Thanksgiving, playing Rummy.

The nine-year-old was awesome. He played the pickup pile on the table and the cards in his hand as well as anyone I had ever played with. His perception of the game was uncanny. I went from thinking about how to help him to trying to figure out how to beat him.

My Dad loved to play Rummy. At 81, he was still a fierce competitor and was just plain lucky with the cards dealt to him or the cards he drew from the deck. No telling how many hours we had played over the years or how many decks of cards we wore out.

It was time for the nine-year-old to go to bed; but not before he beat both of us. My score put me in second place and my son came in dead last. It tickled the grandson to beat both me and his father. He didn't know his great-grandfather was also delighted with his win—neither did my son.

My grandson headed upstairs with his father behind him. It was book time and bedtime.

I looked across the table at my Dad. He had a big smile on his face and a gleam of happiness in his eyes.

"Nothing like family," he said. "Thanks for letting me watch the game. I have to be getting back now. Your mother promised to play cards with me tonight."

A single tear of remembrance rolled down my face and fell on the deck of cards I held in my hand.

THIS MORNING, GOD

The smell of coffee filled the kitchen and wafted into the den. As I sit down at the counter, I think of you. New mornings bring different things for each of us. Today, I will do yard work and later, I will take my truck for an oil change.

Today is another round of chemotherapy for you. Though they consider you terminal, you endure the treatments in hope that they will at least lengthen your days so that you can be with your family a little longer. That's what the doctors tell you and you have to believe them. They are the only game in town.

God sees you this morning, and He also sees me. Omnipotent, Omnipresent, and Omniscient; that's who He is. And because of who He is, I wrote your name on a slip of paper. Next to your name, I place a candle. As I light the candle, I think of you.

Lord, those sparrows that you monitor, and the count that you keep of the hairs on my head show how much you are interested in life as we know it. See the candle, Lord. Zoom in! Note the name that is written there. As surely as the leper wanted and needed cleansing and Blind Bartimaeus needed his sight, my friend needs your touch as well.

Please take a moment and listen as we cry out to You. Hear my prayer and my petition for the only cure available to them. The doctors, much like your disciples who could not cast out the demons, have failed. Cancer is a demon. Throughout your Word, you dispatched demons with ease.

The doctors know their limitations and have proposed a prescription that no pharmacy can fill. If written down, it would read MIRACLE.

See the candle, Lord. Read his name and as you healed the centurion's daughter, please heal my friend today. And Lord, help my unbelief.

MY SAVIOR

Patient and loving, ever-drawing me closer to Him. As I travel through life, He's my constant companion—even when I fail Him. With all my shortcomings, He's always there and forever faithful to me—even when I fail Him

Forgiving on the Cross, forgiving me today, even me. It's impossible to separate myself from His love. It's everlasting, and though I may break His heart, He never stops loving me.

In the manger, He was my Lord. On the cross, He was my Savior. Today, my mainstay, and tomorrow, my Hope.

The shadow of death comes to all men. Like the fourth man walking in the fire, the Son of God will dispel the darkness, and bring me into the eternal light of His presence.

A TIME OF THANKSGIVING

A friend of mine had been estranged from his son for over twenty years. The father and son had previously been close. Business, financial, and legal entanglements breached and destroyed their relationship.

If there was a victim in this fiasco, it was the father. He lost his business and a small fortune, and because of his age, was unable to recover. Forgiving all, he prayed for a miracle of reconciliation.

Holidays, birthdays, and special occasions came and went. His son refused to acknowledge these events and would not return calls or letters.

The father's health deteriorated, and so did his hope for reconciliation. Medical tests revealed a life-threatening problem. The prognosis was not promising.

My friend called to inform me of the situation he was facing and to request that I remember him in my prayers. He sounded happy and upbeat, not concerned or depressed.

I had to ask if the miracle had taken place.

Through tears, he described what transpired. His son was coming every day to check on him and would be with him at the hospital for the procedure. He had hugged his father, kissed him on the forehead and told him he loved him! Prayers had been answered.

God's love is always trying to break down walls and penetrate situations like this one. Broken relationships can be mended and broken hearts can be healed. If we have hope and if we don't despair, miracles can happen.

HIGHWAY ANGEL

Will Johnson was traveling on I-85 and was only two miles from his exit when the traffic slowed and almost came to a standstill. As the traffic inched forward, he was finally able to see the accident. It seemed to involve an eighteen wheeler and several cars. A life-flight helicopter landed and the traffic came to a complete stop. Some people were getting out of their cars and were mingling and talking as the paramedics and emergency personnel did their jobs.

Will got out of his car and leaned against the front fender. He thought about the crash victims and closed his eyes and offered up a prayer that they would be okay. While he was praying, he felt someone touch his arm. He immediately opened his eyes and saw a young man, with shoulder length hair, standing next to him.

"Mind if I pray with you?" the young man asked.

This caught Will off guard, but he immediately regained his composure and said to the stranger, "Not at all. From the looks of the crash site, those folks can use all the prayers they can get."

The young man bowed his head and closed his eyes. Will did the same. Will prayed silently and so did the stranger. After several minutes, Will opened his eyes and the young man was gone. Looking around, he spotted him walking back down the road from the crash site. He came back to where Will was standing and said, "One of the victims isn't going to make it, but the other three will be fine." Will thought this was a strange analysis after such a brief overview of the situation. The young man started a conversation while waiting for the traffic to clear.

"My name is Matthew," the stranger announced, "and I'm heading north looking for work. I'm a construction worker and the economic slowdown and the housing debacle has made construction jobs hard to find. But, being out of work is nowhere near as bad as those in that wreck. We sure do have a lot to be thankful for, not just today, but every day."

Will was impressed, not with the shoulder length hair, but with the prayer, the concern for others, and the thankfulness Matthew seemed to possess. He felt a kindred spirit with him and couldn't figure out why it was so powerful. Then he did something he second guessed all the way home. He spontaneously invited Matthew to have dinner with him and his family.

Matthew accepted the invite, and as the traffic started to move, he went back and got into his car. When the traffic started moving faster and cleared the crash site, Will looked into his rear view mirror and saw Matthew behind him. He called his wife and told her he was bringing a total stranger home for dinner.

"What?" she exclaimed upon hearing how he met the guy. "You're bringing a total stranger to our home just because he impressed you with a prayer offering for the people in a wreck. And, when did you give a pass to long hair? Correct me if I am wrong, but the last time you mentioned long hair on a man, it was in conjunction with the word hippie. Our three grandchildren are here, we're leaving in the morning to take them back to Ohio, and into this mix you bring someone home you found on the highway. Never a dull moment, Will, never a dull moment!"

Matthew's car had seen better days. Will looked up in his rear view from time to time to make sure he was keeping up. He lived in a rural area of the county, about fifteen miles from the interstate.

Apparently Will's wife had informed the grandkids their grandfather was bringing home a total stranger with long hair. Everyone was on the porch waiting for their arrival. Will parked, got of his car and walked back to Matthew's car, to welcome him to his home. The kids walked out into the yard with some reservation, but it disappeared the moment Matthew spoke to them. Will made a mental note that Matthew had a way with making strangers feel as if they already knew him.

The oldest boy had a football in his hand and in no time the three grandkids and Matthew were throwing it to one another and having a great time. Will went into the house and found his wife watching from the kitchen window.

"Looks like you picked a winner," his wife said as Will gave her a hug. "Our grandkids are pretty good judges of character and they definitely like what's his name."

"His name is Matthew," Will told her, "and it's the strangest thing; I feel like I have known him forever. Even the boys seemed to sense the same thing."

After tiring of playing catch with the football, Matthew went to his car and got out a guitar. He came up on the front porch steps and sat down. The grandkids sat down around him. Will came out on the porch to tell them dinner would be ready in about thirty minutes. What he heard was mesmerizing. Matthew had a beautiful voice and played the guitar with so much feeling it seemed as if everything had stopped to listen to him play and sing.

Hearing the music, Will's wife came out and sat down in the swing to listen for a few minutes. Will looked at his wife and when she looked back it was as if to acknowledge that Matthew was indeed special. The boys loved the guitar and sat spellbound by the concert this total stranger was giving to the whole family.

After playing and singing several songs, mostly hymns, Matthew stopped and asked, "Does anyone have a request?" Will's wife had gone in to check on dinner and had just returned to the porch swing.

If Will had been taken in by this stranger, his wife had totally bought in. Immediately she responded and asked Matthew to play and sing "Amazing Grace".

"Sure thing," Matthew responded. The sound of his voice and the way he played the guitar made time seem to stand still.

After dinner, Matthew thanked everyone for their kindness and for opening their hearts and home to a total stranger. No one wanted him to leave, but he insisted he had to get on up the road. But before he left, he asked if he could pray. He prayed and asked God to bless our home and each of us. He called us by name and prayed a hedge of protection around us for our road trip to Ohio.

The "bring a total stranger home" person was so caught up with Matthew, she asked him if he would like to take a few days off from job hunting and vacation with them.

He respectfully declined, hugged each one of us, and left.

When we could no longer see his tail lights, we all were amazed at the void we felt. The grand-boys couldn't believe how much they liked him, and even more, how much they missed him. Will was dumbfounded and his wife said she almost felt depressed and lonely. And all because a total stranger had spent less than five hours with their family.

"Sometimes people are just plain blessings to those who are lucky enough to have them come into their lives," Will told everyone before they retired. "Big day tomorrow, and a long road trip. Who knows, maybe Matthew will stop by again someday when he is passing through this way. Let's get some sleep."

Early the next morning, the Johnson's were on their way to Ohio to return their grandsons to their home. Another tragic accident occurred. This time it involved them. A car with a drunk driver, passed them and cut in too soon, clipping the front fender of Will's car. It was a lonely stretch of a two lane road and there was a drop off at the edge of the pavement. Will's car careened out of control and rolled several times. The drunk driver probably didn't realize what had happened. In any case, he didn't stop.

The next time Will opened his eyes, a nurse was changing his IV. When she saw him open his eyes, she said, "Welcome back stranger."

In a few seconds it all came back and Will remembered the crash. Immediately, he inquired about his wife and grandchildren, and was told his wife was still in the hospital and was about to be sent home. Their son and his wife had come down and picked up the grandchildren and they were all at Will's home. He had been unconscious for three days.

After being examined by a physician, Will asked to see his wife.

"Why don't we bring her to you," the doctor suggested. She is doing well and is about to be released. The doctor told the nurse to get a wheelchair and bring Will's wife to see him.

It was a tearful, but joyous reunion. The grandkids had not sustained serious injury and everyone would recover completely. Will had the worst injuries, and the concussion and subsequent unconscious condition had worried everyone.

His wife filled in all the missing pieces for her husband. "Our car rolled several times and had come to rest upside down. The other driver never stopped. Our car then caught on fire and everyone panicked because it's hard to undo seat belts when you are hanging upside down. The kids managed to get their seat belts unbuckled and then helped me get out of the car. But your weight made it impossible for us to unbuckle your seat belt. Everyone was bleeding and disoriented. Smoke and flames were coming from under the hood and we couldn't get you out. Because you were unconscious you couldn't help yourself, and I made the boys get as far away as possible and flames really started to come from everywhere. The smoke was so heavy we couldn't even see the car. Everyone was hysterical and crying, and that's when we saw him."

"Saw who?" Will asked.

"Matthew," she said. "He walked out of the smoke and he was carrying you in his arms. You suffered no burns, and neither did Matthew. He gently laid you down on the grass and touched each one of us and told us that we would all be fine. Emergency personnel started arriving and no one saw Matthew again. They loaded you up first and got you off to the hospital. We were all hurt, but nothing life-threatening. As they were putting me up in the ambulance, the paramedic told me that he had our guitar and would make sure that it was safe until we were able to go home. I asked him if I could see the guitar and he brought it around to the side door."

"We don't have a guitar," Will observed.

"We do now," his wife responded. "A gift from Matthew, our highway angel."

LOOKING BACK

The morning sun breaks upon another day and finds me in Ohio, a far place from my Enchanted Valley home. I have far less traveling in front of me than behind me. Time, like a conveyor system, moves one along life's highway, allowing reflections of a mirrored past.

I feel as though I have stepped back in time as I drive my son to school. Reality has a way of bringing one's memories into the present and does so again this morning.

Before I get to my son's school, we drop my grandson off at kindergarten. Looking in the rear view mirror at my grandson, and then at my son sitting next to me, makes time warps seem entirely possible. It seemed like only yesterday my son was in kindergarten. When I pulled into the driveway at my grandson's school, for a brief moment, I wasn't sure which one would be getting out— the one next to me or the one in the back seat.

The grandson hugged his dad and told us goodbye and disappeared into the building. I sat there momentarily lost in the memory of another day and another time.

My son, the professor, said, "Let's go, Dad, I have a class to teach in fifteen minutes."

As we drove off he said, "You looked like you were lost in thought back there. What were you thinking about?"

"Just a senior moment," was my reply.

With less road ahead than behind, it helps to lengthen the trip with backward glances into life's rear-view.

PASSING THROUGH

In years past, they called it street preaching. I remember seeing preachers standing on street corners and sometimes on the hood of their car, with Bible in hand, exhorting the Word of God and pleading for lost sinners to come home. Like so many other things, it has vanished from the landscape.

Political correctness has taken over and every decision is based on inclusivity, gender, and diversity. Nothing else matters. This is the new trinity replacing Father, Son, and Holy Spirit. In my corner of the world, political correctness didn't matter; at least to me. My favorite restaurant was filled with like-minded friends who discussed world affairs over a second, a third, and sometimes a fourth cup of coffee. It was a great place to begin your day.

Most of us were past our prime, with less road in front of us than behind us. The majority of us attended one church or the other and were all in agreement about the spiritual condition of our town, our churches, and our nation. In the Good Book, it says that "with the ancient is wisdom, and in length of days, comes understanding" (Job 12:12). That surely fit me and my friends. We knew wisdom always trumped knowledge and common sense would even trump wisdom. There was a general consensus that if most sermons preached on Sunday were medicine, they wouldn't help you, or if they were poison, they wouldn't hurt you.

Our breakfast spot was unique; five booths, eight tables, a counter and two waitresses. There were no murderers among us, no thieves to speak of, no wife-beaters of record, and no complete alcoholics. Just good ol boys, or I guess I should say, good ol men. For about nine dollars, you could get breakfast, all the coffee you could drink, and all the wisdom you could download. Often, you would download a little bull with your wisdom. But it was a fun place to begin your day. That was until he came in one morning.

Whenever the door opened, everyone automatically looked up to see who had come in. This time it was no different, except no one knew the stranger. Every once in a while, someone passing through would stop and have a meal; no big deal. But this morning, everyone knew it was different. The stranger was dressed in faded jeans and a plain, button up shirt. Everyone knew what he carried in his right hand. His clothes were well-worn, but the Bible he carried in his right hand appeared to be worn out many times over. As the door closed behind him, he stopped. He opened the Bible and began to read. "If any man hear my voice and will open the door, I will come in and sup with him and he with me" (Revelation 3:20).

Bill, the owner, and his wife Kristie, were behind the counter. Bill started to go out and address the man, but for some reason, Kristie put a restraining hand on his shoulder. The stranger followed up with two questions. "How many of you here know the Lord Jesus Christ as your personal Savior? If one of you were to die tonight, where would you spend eternity?"

A hush fell over those eating breakfast. The stranger bowed his head, prayed a silent prayer, turned and walked away. Everyone there suddenly had more to contemplate than breakfast. Suddenly, the spiritual trumped the order of the day. The stranger was gone, leaving everyone with something a little more to think about than breakfast with friends.

INSPIRATION OF CHRISTMAS

The last time I was here, the rental house next door was vacant. It's a small house and repairs needing to be made were obvious, even from where I was parked. Next door to the rental house is a business where my wife likes to shop.

I find myself again doing the husband thing—sitting in the car while she shops. Today the house next door has a tenant. A transformation has taken place. The house is the same and the repairs that need to be done are still visible. However, the tenant has been inspired by the season and it's truly amazing what the miracle of Christmas can do, even to an old rental house.

I no longer see paint peeling and boards cracked. I no longer see shingles on the roof needing to be replaced and a window with a broken pane of glass covered with plastic. I see instead the ribbons and bows, placed not in fir or spruce trees, but in crepe myrtles. There is a Frosty in the yard and a small manger scene in a window. One string of Christmas lights is across the front porch.

The brush of Christmas has transformed the ordinary into extraordinary. The imperfections of the rental house are overshadowed by the celebration of the birth of the Christ child. Lives are also changed by this Christ and imperfections and mistakes made in our lives are no longer visible because of the Cross and the forgiveness it extends at Christmas time and all year long.

May the Spirit of Christmas and the Christ of Christmas visit each of us this season, making us more like Him and less like the world we live in.

MIRACLES

In the workshop in the sky where majestic things are done,
Snowflakes are made with precision, exact, and one by one.
The snowflakes are then commissioned to beautify the earth,
With a blanket of purest white, they glisten for all they're worth.
Each snowflake is different and no two are the same,
But some of them are special, and God gives them names.
Sometimes they're given powers, to help those in despair,
Another way the Master shows us just how much He cares.
Jenny was a special snowflake, who was earthward bound,
On a mission of healing-nature, not just to cover the ground.
Floating down from the heavens, guided by the Master's hand,
Feeling humbled for being chosen, for a task so grand.
Her destination sighted, a little cottage in the trees,

Where a broken-hearted Dad, had prayed on bended knees.
His son who had been injured, could not use his legs,
So Dad sent a prayer to God, mercy for his son he begged.
Jenny the special snowflake, didn't make a sound,
As the son sat by the window watching the snow cover the ground.
Jenny landed on the pane of glass right before his eyes,
With a miracle for a cargo, from the Master of the Skies.
The little boy touched the window, not knowing that God was there,
But soon to experience His mercy, as He answered the father's prayer.
As feeling returned to his injured legs, he called for his Dad to come,
But not waiting for his father, through the house he did run.
With tears running down his father's face, they knelt on bended knees,
For God had answered another prayer for all the world to see.

Section 3

THE ANCIENT ORDER OF THINGS

The chatter in the room is subdued and contemplative, respectful but engaging. I'm reminded of words I saw on a headstone: "The ancient order of things."

This is a local breakfast spot where most of the men have long faces and the color of the women's hair point to another time in their lives.

The seasons weigh in heavily on the content of their conversations—spring flowers, August heat, fall colors, and Christmas shopping. Grandchildren are often discussed. And we must not forget politics. This subject can still raise voices and create bulging veins, bringing passion to a boiling point, even in these old vessels.

Picking up bits and pieces of their conversations is as enjoyable as the same breakfast I order every morning. The ancient order of things has dictated I now eat alone. Leaving the restaurant, I think of the Sphinx's riddle, as I listen to the rhythmic tapping on the sidewalk.

SACRIFICE

It was a beautiful backyard. The grass was left plush and deep, allowing the smaller creatures to travel safely and unnoticed. The birds were fed from three different feeders, with sunflower seeds in the feeder by the oak tree and a mixture of seeds in the other two that were located near the goldfish ponds. A small patch of woods bordered the ponds, and many of the animals had homes there. It was a perfect setup.

The squirrels were aggressive with their feeding, but with three feeders, the birds didn't seem to mind. Mr. Smith, the man who lived there, kept the feeders full of seeds at all times and loved to watch the birds and squirrels eat their fill. Nothing was wasted, because whatever managed to fall to the ground was consumed by mice and other smaller creatures venturing out at night. The ponds offered plenty of water for all.

For the most part, the squirrels, birds, and mice got along fine. Ten or so rabbits were also frequent visitors to the backyard and had a warren on the far side of the wooded area.

Mr. Smith had a cat, so over-fed, he never even considered chasing, let alone catching, one of the mice or moles that went their way all over the place without fear or danger. The cat was fat and lazy and his owner was more than generous. Life was good.

Unfortunately, the food chain is larger than mice, squirrels, rabbits, and birds. One morning, a piercing cry was heard from above. It was a sound known to all of the inhabitants of Mr. Smith's backyard. Everyone went scurrying for cover; everyone but Millie. Millie was a sweet little field mouse who was hard of hearing. She never heard the red-tailed hawks cry as he plummeted earthward at a speed over one hundred miles per hour. With pinpoint accuracy, his sharp talons quickly ended little Millie's life.

Everyone loved Millie. Even the squirrels offered their condolences to Marty, Millie's brother, and to Sara, Millie's mother. More than Millie was lost that morning. The tranquility and safety of everyone had been compromised.

Everything has to have sustenance to survive, and the hawk had found a perfect place to live. Creatures know things about each other. Bobby, the leader of the squirrels, noted the hawk didn't have a mate. Since hawks mate for life, Bobby assumed something must have happened to his mate.

In the next few weeks, the hawk wreaked havoc on the population of Mr. Smith's backyard. He didn't discriminate in his hunting or in his choices for dinner. Because of the hawk, everyone was afraid to go out in the daytime. Even the cat, in an unusual outing, was nearly snatched off the ground. The hawk failed to estimate the cat's weight and let him go about four feet into the air.

People who find themselves in difficult situations forget differences and work together for the good of the whole. So it is with animals. They could no longer eat without fear or even go to the pond for water. Six mice, three squirrels, two moles, and three rabbits had already fallen victim to the hawk's insatiable appetite.

Something had to be done quickly. Some were already talking about moving to another place to get away from the on-going carnage. Bobby announced the squirrels were going to have a meeting at night to discuss what could be done, if anything, to rid themselves of this hawk. Everyone was invited. Hawks don't hunt at night, and everyone would be safe since no owls were nearby.

On the appointed night, thirty-three mice, eight rabbits, twelve squirrels, seven moles, a large number of birds and Mr. Smith's cat all came to the meeting. "Desperate times call for desperate action." The moles and mice were a little concerned about the cat's presence, but the cat quickly displayed the talon marks on his back and butt and easily convinced everyone how bad he wanted this feathered monster taken down.

Bobby appointed himself as the moderator and invited any and all to come up with ideas to deal with the hawk. Just the sound of the word *"hawk"* made all the mice shudder. One of the rabbits suggested the cat should do it. After all, the rabbit pointed out, the cat has claws and was bigger than anyone else. The cat quickly pointed out he did not intend to go out again in the daytime, and therefore it was not really his problem. He had come to the meeting only because Bobby had personally invited him. The rabbit evidently had not heard cats have nine lives, or he could have used it in his argument.

It was soon evident no one had the ability, or the nerve, to take on their adversary. Two of the moles had already burrowed back to their homes and some of the mice were preparing to leave. Marty, Millie's brother, asked Bobby if he could speak.

"I have an idea," Marty told the group gathered in the edge of the woods by the pond. "I have given it careful consideration and am prepared both mentally and physically to make sure we take

Millie's killer down. I would like your support, but will do it by myself, if necessary. I'm willing to do this, not only for Millie, but for all who have lost their lives, and for all who remain intimidated by this feathered tyrant."

"No one else has any ideas," Bobby said, "please explain your plan. I'm sure everyone wants to hear your ideas."

Climbing up on the old oak stump, Marty began to explain his plan to the group.

"None of us are physically able to defeat this hawk, and he most certainly isn't going anywhere as long as his food supply lasts. I want all of you to stay out of sight and harm's way for three days. By that time, the hawk should be very hungry. Since we are unable to take him down with external means, I suggest we do it internally. All of the mice are familiar with the poison Mr. Smith puts in his garage. You would think he would wise up, since none of us has ever eaten a single one of those packages. On the morning of the fourth day, I will eat two of them. I will have to eat them quickly before they affect me physically and mentally. I will then go to the bottom of the juniper and run straight out toward the woods. The hawk is always there first thing each morning, and your problems should be over quickly."

Sara had already lost Millie and let out a small cry when Marty suggested giving his life for the group. It didn't seem right she should lose two of her children to this predator. Most everyone was speechless and didn't know how to respond to a sacrifice of this magnitude.

Time seemed suspended as minds and hearts pondered Marty's offer to sacrifice his life for the good of the whole.

The cat spoke first. "This is hero stuff. You, my friend, make me both proud and ashamed at the same time. Proud to know you and ashamed to admit I am too afraid to be that brave."

"Let's meet back here tomorrow night and all of you give me your answer regarding staying out of sight in order to make the hawk hungry enough to do a quick kill," Marty said and then left the group.

News like this travels fast. The next night the woods were full of birds, mice, rabbits, moles, and all matter of creatures who had heard about the brave little field mouse who would take down the predator hawk. The cat was the first one on the scene. It was a party of sorts, a going away party, and a sad gathering, to say the least.

Everyone seemed to bring something to eat and offered it freely to those gathered there. The woods were full of love and mutual respect, one for the other, and a feeling of gratitude to Marty for his bravery, valor, and life he was willing to lay down for the group.

As the time of fellowship drew to a close, Marty thanked everyone for coming and for their help with the hawk. He was the first to leave and no one saw him for the next three days, nor did they know where he went, or what he was doing.

On the morning of the fourth day, Marty returned. He could see the hawk, sitting in his usual place, trying to figure out where his food supply had gone. Marty went quickly to the garage and found two of the packages of poison. He didn't hesitate. Heroes never do. He had spent the last three days reconciling himself with life and death and was prepared to freely give his life for those left and for those already taken— especially for Millie, his sister.

Eating the first bait package quickly, he went to the second one. He could feel the poison taking effect, so he ate the second one without hesitation. He was becoming disoriented and feeling horrible pains in his stomach. Starting for the garage door he stumbled and nearly blacked out. Getting to his feet, he immediately headed for the juniper for protection until he could get into position. He couldn't appear to be sick, because the hawk might not take him. Marty was counting on the hawk's hunger to make a quick and merciful kill.

As he stumbled and staggered through the juniper, he remembered how many times he and Millie had played there in safety. There was a surprise waiting for him at the edge of the cover. Sara, his mother, with tears dripping from her nose, gave him a big hug.

"I am so proud of you," she said, kissing him on the cheek. "We'll never forget you. Tell Millie I love her and I'll see both of you soon."

The poison was doing its job and Marty pulled away from his mother and crept closer to the edge of the juniper. There he was, waiting for someone to make a mistake and become his dinner.

Marty quickly turned and said, "Mom, I love you."

Mustering what little strength he had left, he made a convincing run toward the woods. It was as Marty had predicted, quick and almost painless. The hawk had enjoyed his last meal in Mr. Smith's backyard.

At the edge of the juniper, Sara wept.

MT. ZION

The pastor was late and his tardiness allowed time for a sobering walk up the hillside. I didn't need a compass to determine which direction was East. All the headstones and markers faced that way. Hope is ever present, even in cemeteries.

A recent burial was indicated by fresh flowers and earth recently turned. A new neighbor had moved into what appeared to be a very old neighborhood. Graves dating from the early 1800's were everywhere.

Markers were so old some names and dates were obliterated. Time, the very commodity each one residing here ran out of, is now so brazen as to take away their identities.

As I read names and dates, I tried to imagine the era in which they lived and died. What, according to my memory of history, was happening in 1803, 1835, 1856, and all of the other by-gone years.

As I stood in front of Ezekiel Brown's final resting place, my cell phone rang, breaking the silence of eternity being contemplated. I was somewhere between his birth in 1807, and his death in 1886. Why did I answer my cell phone? Habit, I guess. It was someone doing marketing for a surveillance equipment company. After several no's, they finally hung up. But Ezekiel had closed the door and wouldn't allow me back inside. I couldn't blame him. Rude is rude no matter the century. I moved on.

Ezekiel had a neighbor, a small neighbor, and I decided to read her poetry cut deep into the headstone: *"Only five years with us she spent, till God for her His angels sent."* No doubt Elizabeth had brought lots of joy and happiness into her family that sixth day of January, 1929. The Stock Market would crash later that year. It was not the best of years to be born. But the crash of the market paled in comparison to January 25, 1934, when Elizabeth moved here permanently.

"Who wept for this child?" I thought.

"I did and still do," came a voice into my mind.

I looked next door and there was her mother's place. Both mother and daughter, side by side, separated only by a few feet of earth and eternity.

The hillside seemed alive.

"Come here."

"No, over here. Come over here and read my name."

"Please say my name. I haven't heard it in so long."

I went to as many as I could, saying each one aloud and reading the birth dates. I purposely did not read the date of their death. Many of the stones were so old and worn I could not read their names.

I felt their pain, the pain of being nameless and forgotten.

I heard the pastor as he arrived in the parking lot. I could feel the disappointment of those whose names I had not read.

"I will come back," I told them. "I will come and visit you again."

ONE MORE TIME

Though the parking lot was full, people still drove through in hopes of finding a place. This was, after all, the premier spot to see the massive fireworks display put on every Fourth of July by the resort. Knowing that, we arrived early, parked and got our chairs set up and our snacks out. We were ready.

The car next to us assumed everyone in the parking lot was a fan of country music. Johnny Cash, though dead, sang his heart out. "I can hear that train a coming" echoed throughout the valley. It was a four wheel drive, jacked up SUV juke box with a real live wannabe DJ.

Some kids had sparklers and their parents looked very irresponsible. Both parents were smoking and paid little attention to their kids or the sparklers. They would throw them up in the air and the parents weren't the least bit concerned about where the sparklers would land. I assumed one would eventually find its way to the hood of my car and leave a permanent burn mark to remember this happy occasion of our nation's birthday.

There is a book that makes reference to old age by saying "with the ancient is wisdom and in length of days comes understanding" (Job 12:12). Some of us get smarter with age, and unfortunately, some of us get cynical and grouchy. I have acquired at least three of those qualities.

As I observed the different vehicles parked around us, I saw all levels of economic achievement gathered here. One, assuming he has gotten smarter with age, could possibly observe the people and match them up with their vehicle. I'm not sure if that is wisdom gathered through the aging process or one being cynical because my attendance was mandatory. It would be fair to say all social classes had come out to enjoy the fireworks display and to celebrate the Fourth of July.

The one thing not separated by position or economic status was the children. For the most part, all were playing together happily, awaiting the fireworks which would begin at nightfall. Some parents anxiously watched their children at play, and some did not appear to watch their children at all. Children are God's blessing to all of us and His reminder of who we should be every day.

The combined age of my group is two hundred and twenty years. There are only three of us; two are sixty four and one is ninety two years old. Do the math. I have gotten to the place where some things fall into this category—if you have seen one fireworks display, you have seen them all.

This is a kid's thing, I told myself, like gathering around a Christmas tree. It means more to the children, and rightly so.

As the darkness gathered around us, the level of anticipation grew appreciably. Parents picked up their small children and started pointing to the area that would soon explode with brilliance and fill the night sky with wonder. Oohes and ahs and peels of children's laughter would soon follow each starburst and boom.

Whatever fool said, "if you have seen one fireworks display you've seen them all" was mistaken. Two hundred and twenty years of living, all wrapped up in three people, oohed and aahed along with the children.

CHEATED

The sun tiptoed into the house, quietly sneaking in around the closed blinds and drapes, transforming the darkness into light. Their health had declined, but their marriage of fifty six years bound them together in a testament of all the good, love and life has to offer.

A stroke had affected her speech and two heart surgeries had slowed him down considerably. Now they spent a lot of time reading and only went out occasionally. In the mornings, they would lie in bed and he would recant their travels or perhaps things they had enjoyed together. She could still speak, but it was laborious and hard to understand. She would listen and smile at his animated tales of yesterday, and sometimes he told it as she remembered it, but often he would embellish the stories and make them even more fun to remember.

"Remember when we went to Ireland?" he asked her. "Remember when we went to the Falconry and I flew the falcon. He must have had a twenty foot wingspan. No, scratch that. His wingspan was thirty feet, if it was as inch."

"Remember when we told your father we wanted to get married? We were both scared silly. Had no idea how he would respond. I grew to love that old fart, almost as much as I loved my own father." This morning, the sun continued its mission and daylight had found the two life-time lovers lying in bed. He rolled over and put his arm around her. His eyes, filled with tears, emptied onto the pillow case when he turned over to face her. Her eyes were open and he wept as he snuggled up next to her cold, lifeless body.

"You know this isn't right," he said. "It wasn't supposed to be like this. I don't want to call the kids and I sure don't want to call EMS, but I have to. You'd do the same thing, wouldn't you? There's no option here, but I can't imagine our home without you in it. I was supposed to go first. I had the bad ticker, but damned, if you didn't pull a fast one on me. Honey, go slow and look over your shoulder often. I'm coming, I promise you. See you soon."

SHOES

The shoes are 90-years-old, give or take a few months. Red clay, indicative of the South, dried brick-hard on the sole of the left shoe. I don't know where his first pair of leather shoes found the red clay—perhaps on the dirt streets of his neighborhood.

Other shoes would take him many places. In the 1930s, education wasn't stressed in poorer economic areas. Before he dropped out of school, his shoes would carry him to the front of his second-grade class to receive a plastic duck, a prize for making excellent grades. In the sixth grade, he would journey to Atlanta to represent his county as their marble champion, but would lose in the first round of the tournament. In the seventh grade, he would walk away from education forever.

His shoes would serve him well on his first job delivering telegrams for Western Union by bicycle. A local train wreck would require him to cover over twelve miles, one way, to deliver a telegram. He told the story many times, leaving the listener with a visual image of the engine lying on its side, and the cars strewn helter-skelter, on either side of the tracks.

In 1940, dress shoes would take him in front of the Justice of the Peace for his wedding. Work shoes would be worn out many times over, as he labored year after year in a textile mill, in order to provide for the family that soon followed his marriage.

In 1942, he traded his work shoes in for combat boots, and

tramped all over Europe with the Third Army. His outfit would be one of the first to enter Berlin. He always declined to talk about the specifics of war, saying nothing good could ever come from it.

He would return home in 1945 and trade the combat boots in for more work shoes. Many pairs would be worn out in the textile industry before he retired. Another pair of dress shoes would take him to an event with his wife of fifty-five years; her funeral.

Fewer shoes would be worn out in the last ten years of his life due to foot problems. Tennis shoes with Velcro were his choice in later years. Due to loneliness, those tennis shoes would visit many friends and former mill hands often carrying those unable to drive to the doctor, to get groceries, or whatever they needed.

Cancer came calling and didn't care about shoes, past or present. Dad moved in with us, and in time, could not bathe himself. I learned something important about his feet which filled a life time of assorted shoes.

Helping him shower, he informed me I forgot to wash between his toes. I thought he was joking, but he wasn't. Not only did I have to wash between his toes every time he showered, I had to dry between them as well. Cancer doesn't tell jokes or laugh, but we laughed often about shower-time.

I would say, "Come on Dad, let's go wash between your toes."

Dress shoes would be required again. This time, I would wear them, and walk beside his casket to his final resting place next to Mom.

ANOTHER PLACE AND ANOTHER TIME

Cub scouts met one Thursday night a month and the dad made it an evening out with his son; a hike, weather permitting, dinner, and then the scout meeting. This week the weather didn't cooperate, and they finished dinner earlier than usual. They had about forty-five minutes before the scout meeting began and wondered what they could do.

The father spotted a department store and asked his son if he would like to look at some toys. Christmas was just five weeks away and his son brightened up and smiled at the thought of shopping for toys. It wasn't the neighborhood they lived in, or shopped in, and the vehicles in the parking lot said volumes about the financial condition of the customers.

The father was quite successful and had earned his PhD from a very well known university. He had already published several books and created quite a demand for his services, lecturing at conferences and at other universities. He was happily married with three children. Life was good.

The surrounding neighborhood wasn't a place to experience car trouble, or be stranded at night. Parking their very nice vehicle close to the building, they got out and entered the store.

At six-years-old, the son didn't notice the difference in the way he was dressed compared to the other kids who were also looking at toys. They were all excited and interacted like they were, and always had been, best of friends.

A strange thing happened as the father watched his son and the other kids looking at the Christmas possibilities Santa might bring them. He looked back. Back to another place and time, back to another store just like this one, in another neighborhood, just like this one, and with other people, just like these people.

These other people had names. He called them Nanny and Papa and he spent lots of time with them. They were his favorite grandparents. Both had quit school in the seventh grade and had worked in textile mills their entire lives. They had written no books, lectured to no one, and had struggled their whole lives to make ends meet. Good, hardworking people just like the ones shopping here. Perhaps some of these children playing with his son were here with their grandparents. He had often gone to a store just like this one, with his Nanny and Papa, and invariably, they would always buy him something.

He thought of the toys his children already had at home. In reality, they didn't need anything from Santa. Santa could restock from their toy boxes and they would never miss a thing. It was time to leave in order to make the Cub Scout meeting. He told his son to tell his new friends goodbye and they started to the car.

As they walked through the store, the father was somehow different. He no longer saw any disparity in the surroundings. Entering the parking area, he only saw cars, not status symbols. He felt a loving presence from his past and had a warm feeling in his heart.

HIT AND RUN

As her children crossed the road, the mother watched in horror as a speeding car topped the hill. The only thing she could do was stand there, paralyzed with fear.

The driver never applied his brakes and ran down the three youngsters who were in his path. Failing to stop to offer assistance, he sped away as if nothing had happened.

One was killed instantly, and two more lay dying on the asphalt. The mother couldn't do anything to help them. With her two remaining children, and a grieving heart, she turned and walked back into the woods.

No one ever said life was fair, but tragedies like this happen far too often in the lives of possums, who are only trying to cross the road.

SOUND OF SILENCE

Sometimes the noise in my favorite restaurant is deafening, with people talking, laughing, and visiting with one another over breakfast or lunch. Sometimes it's hard to hear the conversation at your table because everyone has to increase the volume in order to be heard.

This morning, I went for breakfast. The main crowd had already come and gone, and it was relatively quiet. The people at the table in the corner were laughing a lot and apparently enjoying themselves. Real laughter is infectious. Except for the laughter, not a sound came from this group. None of them could talk very loud; in fact, they couldn't speak at all.

The laughter was being generated from conversation through sign language. While I can't sign, I do enjoy genuine laughter. It made me wish I knew what was so funny. There would be peals of laughter, accompanied with great facial expressions. All four were very adept with signing, and like with verbal conversations, they all seemed to sign at the same time.

The waitress knew them, and they were able to communicate with her. Normally, I would have felt compassion for them, but not today. This was the happiest group I had been around in a long while, and as I looked around at the others eating in the restaurant, I believe they were as inquisitive as I was as to the content of their conversation. They were also jealous of such pure joy. I know, because I was too.

THIS WAS THEN

A man in an old station wagon canvassed our neighborhood offering to paint house numbers on the curb, using white numbers with a blue-blocked background. A second option was to paint the house number on a brick. The brick would be painted blue and the numbers would still be in white. The cost of either option was five dollars. Almost every one of our neighbors became a customer of this freelance entrepreneur. But, not my Dad. He said our house number was already on the house, and anyone looking for us, already knew where we lived.

My best friend lived two doors up the street. His house was easy to find because he had a blue brick in the front yard with his house number painted on it in white. Across the street and two doors up from my friend lived Carolyn. She drove a burgundy Comet and wore the shortest skirts in the neighborhood. We made sure we were sitting on my friend's front steps everyday when she arrived home from work.

Sometimes, we would find ourselves walking up the street just as she would make her exit from her car. We were fifteen years old and coming of age. Jeannie C. Riley's, Harper Valley PTA, was at the top of the charts and our testosterone was getting there.

Carolyn remained my friend for the rest of her life. I later shared with her our daily vigil of her exit from her car, and whenever it was brought up, we would both have a good laugh. Her skirts had gotten longer, and she had gained a considerable amount of weight. My testosterone had peaked and declined in what seemed like a few short years. She died an early death and I attended her funeral. My short-skirt watching associate didn't attend her funeral. He had attended his own a few years earlier.

As I drive down to my old home town, I share with my wife these stories of blue bricks, short skirts, and friends I can no longer visit. I found myself again involved with the marking of where someone would live. This time, it would be a permanent address. It would be black marble from India, not a hand painted blue brick, and would cost a lot more than five dollars.

My Dad and Mom's place is directly behind ours. They've already moved in; we will in due time. About two doors up and across the grass is the lady with the once short skirts and burgundy Comet. I don't know where Jeannie C. Riley or my best friend is today. It doesn't really matter because there are no steps here to sit on.

EMPTY NEST

There is something magical about springtime. It's a resurrection of sorts—a coming-out party for many outside plants hiding beneath mulched flower beds to escape the shadows cast by winter. Everything knows it's a happening. Naked trees start to reclothe themselves and grasses begin to regain their color. All creatures, great and small, start families. It's a good time for the earth and all her inhabitants.

About a week after moving our plants from the basement to the front porch, I noticed a pair of birds had selected a hanging fern for their nesting site and another pair had selected a large potted plant for their new family home. The fern was on the end of the porch and the potted plant was on a stand, immediately by our front door.

Each morning, my wife and I would sit in the front porch swing and drink our coffee. The birds didn't seem threatened by our presence and went about building their nests as if we weren't even there. We enjoyed watching them ferry precious building materials and labor tirelessly in their endeavor. I told my wife the mother bird's clock was ticking, and not getting the new nest completed wasn't an option they could entertain. Having an active imagination, I imagined hard hats, safety glasses, and safety shoes for the little birds. I told my wife if she would listen closely, she could hear the sound of their hammers and saws. She checked my coffee cup to make sure I was drinking only coffee.

I wondered if the two pair of birds knew each other or if they communicated at night when building had to cease. I wondered why one pair had picked the fern in the hanging basket and the other pair had picked the potted plant by the door. I wondered if the male had any input in the selection site—probably not.

Timing is everything. No sooner than the nests were completed, eggs were laid. Oddly, the nest in the hanging fern only had one egg. The other nest had five. I wondered why.

We watched both pair of birds take turns minding the nests. We felt like we were expectant parents and couldn't wait to see the baby birds. I had to be careful watering the plants. The birds residing in the hanging basket were not as acceptable of us as the ones in the flower pot by the door. The ones by the doorway would not leave the nest, even when I watered the plant. We could get fairly close and even ask them how it was going and they seemed to be receptive to our interest in their family and to our conversation. However, they never did respond.

In no time at all, five little fuzzy heads were in one nest and one little fuzzy head was in the other. It seemed sad that one had to be all alone.

How quickly they grew. In a short time, the nest of five was a nest of five large mouths—always open and always hungry. They would pick up the vibration of movement on the porch and immediately think it was meal time. The mother and father worked overtime to take care of them and I likened it to a family having to work two jobs to make ends meet.

The nest of one must have felt spoiled. He grew very fast because all of the food went into his mouth. I told my wife I felt sorry for him. He had no idea what it was like to share, to feel siblings next to him on a cool night, or to chirp in unison when Mom or Dad appeared with dinner.

The two families of birds represented life to me. Choices always dictate outcome. One family leisurely raising one child, and another family struggling to feed five. There was no right and wrong here, just two different families on two different paths.

My wife and I were caught up with our extended feathered families. The dynamics of a family of seven and a family of three were intriguing. Both seemed to be working it out just fine.

I wondered if the adult birds from both families ever sat on our swing at night and compared notes or shared a little down time while all their children were asleep. No way, I told myself. The parents of the five were too exhausted to visit. They just wanted to rest and get ready for the next day's feeding.

One morning, we were devastated. We knew it was coming, but had refused to discuss it. We had experienced it twice before and didn't want to think about it happening to us again.

They were all gone—both families had left and not even bothered to tell us goodbye. We looked around in the shrubs and flower beds, hoping maybe some of the young ones were still close by. No luck.

We stood for a moment by the nest which had been the crowded home of five—so barren and empty, no pushing, or crowding, no competing for the next bite of food, no nothing.

A single tear ran down my wife's face. I took her hand and we went back inside to our own empty nest.

THREE A.M.

Three A.M. finds me at the kitchen counter with a freshly brewed cup of coffee in my hand. I couldn't sleep. The fridge hums contently doing its thankless job. The only other sound comes from the wall clock. The pendulum makes an ever so soft tick-tock as it keeps time for the humming fridge.

Some nights I see my neighbor's lights through the kitchen window. But not this night. What is, what was, and what might have been didn't visit him tonight.

Finishing my second cup, the fridge decides to rest for a while. The clock's pendulum, however, does not. It faithfully continues to mark the passing of a life well spent, sitting at the kitchen counter, drinking coffee and remembering what is, what was, and what might still be.

TRAGEDY ON CROOKED CREEK

It was bitter cold. Nightfall was coming fast and if he couldn't find shelter, he would freeze to death. An injured foot made movement slow. Just as he was about to resign himself to a night outside in sub-freezing temperatures, he spied an open door with no one around. Sanctuary, just in the nick of time.

He slipped inside, unnoticed. He had no shoes, and walking on the cold concrete floor sent a shiver throughout his entire body. He was so cold that coherent thoughts refused to materialize. He tried to remember the last time he had slept with a roof over his head. Usually, he would drift off to sleep under a canopy of stars. But not tonight; Lady Luck had smiled big time, and he was very thankful.

It was a large room of sorts and dimly lit by a single light. Across the room, piles of newspapers and old clothes were stacked in the corner. This would be a good place to bed down, with less chance of being discovered. The only thing bothering him more than the cold was the intense pain in his stomach. It seemed like an eternity since his last meal.

Hearing voices and footsteps, he darted into the shadows. Someone opened another door and stepped out on the cold, concrete floor. He could make out two people discussing something, but he couldn't understand what they were saying. He waited quietly in his hiding place. He must not be discovered because he couldn't bear the thought of being chased outside into the cold.

The big man was holding something in his hand. After leaning over and placing the object on the floor, he said something to the other person, laughed, and started back inside the house. As he turned to enter the house, he noticed the garage door was open. Quickly closing the door, he paused a moment to look around to make sure everything was in order. Satisfied all was well, they went back inside the house.

With both doors closed, he was trapped inside. This was not a bad problem to have considering the temperature outside.

The smell of food teased his nostrils and he thought he was hallucinating. But no, the scent was real. Where was it coming from? It seemed to be coming from the other doorway. Leaving the safety of his corner, he carefully crossed the room. He saw the object the man had placed on the floor. He knew it; he knew his senses weren't wrong. Why would anyone put cheese on the floor? This was indeed his lucky night—shelter and his favorite food. His hunger was so intense, his mind could not reason.

As he took the morsel of food, the cold night and his intense hunger vanished forever. The tightly wound spring released the cold, steel bar. No one heard the click as the trap worked to perfection. No one heard the half-scream forever lodged in his throat, unable to escape.

WIND

Crepe myrtles perform a syncopated waltz, while hanging ferns turn right, then left. Giant trees line dance in place as inanimate objects shuffle down the street. Someone stops suddenly and zips their coat. Children on a playground—seen, but not heard. A flag snaps to attention, over and over. A cat sits and watches anxiously. A woman's fingers press hard against the window pane. Remembering, remembering, remembering.

MILLIE

In the best of circumstances, life never exceeds more than six months. Weaned from their mother, they are usually sold at ten to twelve weeks of age. They will never see her again.

Bloodlines matter, but not to the pigs.

They will go to new homes where lots of special care and attention will be given to them. They will be well fed, brushed, weighed and pampered their entire life.

The ticking clock uses up six months of ticks all too quickly. Before the pigs realize it, it's showtime at the fair.

While bedded down in their holding pens, they visit with other pigs. They all have one thing in common; this will be their only fair.

Their time in the show ring will be brief. A second trip is scheduled immediately following the judging. The hands that pampered them will do so no more. No one will ever again call them by their given names.

They made the trip to the fair as royalty. Their trip from the fair will be mass transit. They came from separate homes, made friends in adjoining pens, and will travel to their final destination together–the place of the eternal scream.

THE PLANTER

The house, void of shadows, stands watch over-looking flowers planted and dreams vanquished. Spring is evident as the landscape comes to life, in tribute to what would not be not for the planter, not this season.

Misfortune, choices, or circumstances of the times had extinguished the fire and soul of the planter, yielding the house void of shadows and empty.

Sadness hangs in the air, as if in remembrance of the one who had lived there.

Shrubs and flowers bloom, but not for the one who selected and placed them in the landscape. Strawberries and blueberries will be harvested by strangers who did not plant them. The strangers dream their own dreams, enjoying the fruits of another's labor, while the planter harvests his own crop of misery and misfortune.

THE OTHER SIDE

His world had been turned upside down. The six-figure plus job which had fueled his family's lifestyle had disappeared through corporate downsizing. Economics can be a bitch.

Foreclosure took their beautiful home. Both their expensive cars had been replaced by one, fifteen-hundred-dollar clunker. Somehow, the old car made the weekly trips to the food pantry a little more tolerable. The antiquated two bedroom mobile home didn't seem to mind the relic being parked next to it. As a matter of fact, they made a good pair.

The wife and two children were gone. She couldn't take it any longer. The economic circle she had been jettisoned from had been her life. Some of her closest friends had reached out to help, but she had refused their offers.

She had refused to ride in the clunker and wouldn't go anywhere near the food pantry. Her family had always been affluent and still was. The smell of money and the lure of nice things had drawn her back home to her family. She had taken their children with her.

His pain had also been great, and his pride had suffered far too much to go back home to her family. He no longer felt guilty for their economic situation. As a matter of fact, he no longer felt anything.

There were no prospects for a job that would support them in the manner they had become accustomed to and the lifestyle his wife demanded. Contentment can be found in the bottom of a wagon rut, if one is willing to look for it and accept it, he thought.

He drove the clunker to a local beach and parked it next to the playground.

He had left a note in the mobile home for his landlord with instructions to send all his money to his children. He included their address and the location of what would be the only inheritance they would receive from their father; eighty-three dollars and twelve cents under the floor mat on the passenger side of his car. The clunker would be parked at the local beach.

Walking past the playground, he ventured to the lone point of the park and sat down in a swing. It was a hot July day, but the trees provided shade, and the breeze coming from the lake, made it very comfortable. Best of all, it was free.

It was the Fourth of July and a boat parade had started its procession around the lake. All of the boats were decorated with patriotic themes and the passengers waved enthusiastically. He thought briefly about the nation's birthday, and realized he too, would have something in common with her on this Fourth. He remembered their boat and all the happy times the family had enjoyed on this very lake.

He felt obligated to wave at the first few that came by. They were so happy and full of life and were clearly celebrating with patriotic fervor. Then the waves, lapping lazily at the rocky shoreline, caught his attention and reminded him of his reason for being at the lake.

The boat parade had been over for a while. He continued to watch the waves. They were no longer slapping the rocks as they had earlier. They gently lapped at the shoreline before disappearing back into the whole.

Standing up, he looked across the lake at the distant mountain range bordering the far shore. "Surely things will be better on the other side," he said aloud as he entered the water. Swimming had never been his forte.

TECHNOLOGY

Technology is great, but stop fooling yourself. Only a small handful of people really give a tinker's damn about you, your dog, or even your children. They may like your stuff, but if that makes you feel good, you need some serious help. However, the few people in your life who really care about you, your dog and your children, deserve far more than a post on Facebook, a text message, or a convenient email. They need to see you and hear your voice as often as possible. Facebook, email, and texting cannot be accessed from the grave. Only close encounters of the family kind will be remembered.

THE OLD MAN AND THE BEE

Leaves dance to the gentle breeze blowing across the lake. The beach is empty–a solitary boat crosses the vast expanse of water. No laughter coming from the playground–no creaking swings. Seven geese, going somewhere, swim by. Why seven, and not six or eight? Seven is an odd number, but so is one.

A honey bee, normally unwanted company, offers companionship today. And I need that. Landing on the open pages of my book, and even on my hand, he too, seems lonely. Fall is in the air—what will happen to the honey bee?

White, thinning hair, easily bruised skin, bad knees—what will happen to me? A single honey bee and a lonely old man, enjoying the last days of summer together.

PATIENCE

As I sit on my deck, I watch the squirrel attacking the bird feeder, taking that which does not rightfully belong to him. The birds watch and wait their turn. They know the ravenous squirrel cannot possibly consume all the seed. He will soon tire, and having eaten his fill, will move on, allowing the birds their turn. It is, after all, their feeder.

Time passes slowly when one is practicing patience. The squirrel eats his fill and then hangs upside down on the feeder, as if to taunt the birds. Finally, he drops to the ground and disappears into the woods.

The birds, having waited patiently, converge on the feeder, thankful for their turn.

FAMILY TREE

The old oak tree is sad today and I believe she knew
That this was it, the final day, her living days were through.
Four generations of children, she shaded them with care,
Lots of tire swings, and climbing, as high as they would dare.
The wind, the ice, the lightning, had done their very best,
But the old oak tree showed her power, withstanding all their tests.
But time has caught up with the old oak tree and she can no longer hold her own,
And when the high winds break a limb, you can almost hear her groan.
I look at her with pity as she towers towards the sky,
And try to justify it, that everything must die.
Her big limbs creaked from a gentle breeze and I swore I heard her say,

Find something else better to do, don't do this today.
I started to feel like a villain, holding an instrument of death,
And a chill ran through my body and my thoughts turned to myself.
When time has taken its toll on me and my useful days are past,
Would anyone have the right to decide which day would be my last?
Stepping back from the old oak tree, I smiled and said you win,
But you know as well as I do, that the day will come again.
Continue to stand magnificently as long as you possibly can,
And the day you fall will be natural, and not brought about by man.

TIME

Midday marks the passing, from morning to evening time,
The past and future meet here in furrows of the mind.
Sweet fragrances of memories past edge right up to the line
As midday marks the passing, from morning to evening time.
The future demands boldness while drawing strength from the past
New horizons beckon to us, but their newness will not last.
As timelines in life are noted, and challenges conquered there
The future becomes the past, both handled with great care.
Midday comes to quickly, mornings pass, it's evening time,
Sweet fragrances of memories past come now and cross the line.
The mark, that line once so distinct blends now and is hard to see
As fragrances of memories past flood my future thoughts for me.

AMEN & AMEN

Bubba was down on his luck again. The only place in town for high school dropouts to work had just closed its doors. Most of his friends worked in the plant with him, and now they all stood in the company parking lot, unemployed. An hour had passed and no one wanted to leave, because leaving meant going home and telling their families about losing their jobs. And to make matters worse, if that were possible, it was just twenty-three days until Christmas.

His friends were just like him. They had attended the same high school, played football and baseball together, and also like him, had dropped out of school and started working in the furniture plant which had just closed down. They had all married young and had two or three kids each. They had no money to speak of, living from paycheck to paycheck.

Hunting and fishing together in the local woods and streams was their idea of a country club membership. And, grilling out together on weekends, well, it just couldn't get any better than that. Beer, dogs, burgers and horseshoes—what more could a man want? The finest restaurants in New York never served such delicious fare as they cooked on their backyard grills.

Bubba and his friends had one other thing in common—they all lived in Eula's Trailer Park. A few of them actually owned their trailers and rented their lots from Eula, but most rented their trailers as well.

Eula was one of them. She was a good ole girl and easy to work with. She had quit school the same year Bubba did. At the time, Eula had been pregnant and so had Clarice, Bubba's girlfriend. Clarice got Bubba, but Eula got lucky. The reason Eula got lucky was because William, the father of her child, had a full ride to Harvard. William's father was president of the biggest bank in the county and he wasn't about to let a local ruin his son's future. Eula gave William's dad a nickname; she called him Bank Daddy.

After Bank Daddy found out about the pregnancy, he decided to handle the situation the only way he knew how. Throw money at it. The trailer park had been repossessed, and a back room deal was made between Bank Daddy and Eula's father. This is a familiar story. Eula got the trailer park, and Bank Daddy's son got to go to Harvard, free and clear of any paternity issues.

He never knew William continued to see Eula. Whenever he came home from college, he would meet her at a small motel across the mountain. She never told her little Billy who his father was, or made any excuses for his non-existence. She never married; neither did William. Apparently, there had been more to the high school fling than a full ride to Harvard could erase. Bubba often wondered why she remained single, but locals usually mind their own business.

Back in the parking lot, Bubba and his friends were in panic mode. What were they going to do for a job? There was nothing in the area. The closest opportunity for work was seventy or so miles away on the other side of the mountain. And, their biggest problem was Christmas. Where would they get money for Christmas, just a few weeks away?

All of a sudden, Bubba, who had been sitting on the tailgate of his Chevy pickup, jumped up and startled the others with an announcement.

"I know what we can do. We'll go see Eula. She knows stuff and has a good business head on her shoulders. She'll know what to do."

Everyone agreed, and one after another, the pickup trucks

roared to life. It looked like a parade, as Chevys and Fords left the parking lot headed for Eula's. A faint sound of country music could be heard over the barking tailpipes.

Eula had a double-wide parked on Lot One. It served as her home, and was also the trailer park office. She was sitting at her desk when Bubba and his entourage turned in and braked hard.

Recognizing something had happened, she hurried out on the deck to meet her tenants, who were also her friends. Bubba got to the deck first. She could see the stress on his face.

"What's wrong, Bubba" Eula said as she put her hand on his shoulder.

"We just lost our jobs, and the plant's closing for good. We have to find new jobs, but we also have Christmas breathing down our necks. If it wasn't so scary, it'd be funny and we could sing Haggard's song about making it through December. But this ain't funny and we don't know what to do. Got any ideas?"

By now, everyone was on the deck. Some leaned against the community hot tub, and others against the deck railing. Taking a deep breath, Eula sat down in a deck chair.

"Give me a few minutes," she told them. "There's beer in the fridge. LJ, go get us a beer and we'll think this thing out together."

Little Jimmy went inside Eula's trailer, and in a few minutes, returned with an armful of beer.

The tabs were pulled-up in unison, all except Eula's. She sat in the deck chair with her hands behind her head. Her beer remained unopened. She had a faraway look the boys hadn't seen before. She had done well, and the trailer park had made her quite a living. She was remembering less fortunate times, and her heart ached for the boys sitting in front of her, waiting for her answer to their tragic situation.

"Life's not fair," she finally said.

"Tell us something we don't already know," Bubba said and half-heartedly tried to smile.

"Y'all already know what has to be done about the jobs. There's nothing left here if the plant stays closed. You'll have to go over the mountain. Maybe y'all can find jobs close together and carpool. That'll help a little. But Christmas, that's the big problem we have to deal with first."

"Twenty three days away and none of us have bought much of nothing, and you know we ain't got no money stashed away," Bubba said as spokesperson for the group.

There were nods all around in agreement.

"Wait just a minute," Eula said with a smile creeping across her face. Jumping up from the deck chair, she disappeared into the trailer and returned with a brochure.

"Here's the answer," Eula proclaimed, as she handed it to Bubba.

Bubba looked puzzled, but passed it around for the rest of the guys to see. No one looking at the brochure seemed to see an answer to their problem. It announced the annual tour of homes in town. It took place every Christmas, but no one from the trailer park ever bothered to go.

Bubba was the first one to question her sanity. He called the rich people in town, with the big homes, *hootie tooties,* and couldn't see how paying to go see their homes would help with their Christmas or with paying their lot rent at the trailer park.

"What's this got to do with our problem?" asked Little Jimmy.

"Just hear me out, boys. Here's what we're gonna do. They charge twenty dollars to do their tour of homes and believe me, it generates tons of money. We'll host our own tour of homes here at the trailer park. We'll charge thirty dollars because most of the ones coming here have never seen inside a trailer home before. We'll make a killing, and it may be the best Christmas y'all have ever had."

"Have you been drinking this morning?" Bubba asked her. "It's awful early to be hitting the hard stuff."

"You know I don't drink hard stuff," Eula laughed, as only she could laugh.

"The hootie tooties aren't going to pay us to see inside our trailers," Little Jimmy said. "Hell, they're scared to drive into the park. They sure ain't gonna get out and come in."

"I agree," Bubba said. "They wouldn't be caught dead in our trailers, let alone pay us to come inside and look around."

"You leave them coming to me," Eula said. "They'll come, come gladly, and be even more happy to pay us. Here's what I want y'all to do. Let's clean this place up. Get all the trash picked up, get all the decks pressure washed and get the inside of your trailers spic and span. Let's put up extra decorations at the entrance and I have garland for the office trailer. I want this place to look like Vegas on a dark night. If the weather's good, we'll even let them play trailer park horseshoes. Hell, we might even charge extra for that."

"And Bubba, we're gonna have beer, dogs, and burgers to die for. And most of all, I want y'all to be to them, what you are to me—good ole boys. Just be yourself and tell your families to do the same. Everyone at Eula's is a class act, and it's past time the townspeople realized it. They will absolutely love us. This could turn into an annual event—Christmas at the Trailer Park."

"Why are y'all just standing around?" she said as she started inside. "I'm going to town to get the flyers printed up. Y'all better get this place shipshape. We want the townsfolk to have a good experience on their first visit to our homes."

As Eula backed out of her parking place next to her doublewide, the boys were still standing stupefied at the back of Bubba's truck. They looked like little boys, not like unemployed fathers and husbands. She not only felt their pain, it was visible as well. Eula let her window down and put a triumphant fist in the air and yelled *"Yes"* loud enough for them to hear her.

Two hours later, when she returned, the boys were still standing around, feeling sorry for themselves. Even though they thought she had lost her mind, they still trusted her. After all, she had taken a little bit of promiscuity and turned it into quite a bit of prominence, at least in their eyes.

As she walked past them, she gave them the "what's this" gesture with her hands. She planned to address them in a little while, but for right now she needed to get in her office and make a list of people to call on. She already knew the list would be short. It would only have one name–Bank Daddy. It was the only name she needed. He'd do all the grunt work for her, making sure everyone came and insuring the first annual Trailer Park Tour of Homes would be a tremendous success.

In a moment of weakness, on one of William's return rendezvous with Eula, he had confided a very intimate secret about his dad. If it went public, it would ruin his career and jeopardize his community standing. Eula smiled. This couldn't miss.

The next day, after picking up the flyers, she went straight to the bank. There was other financial institutions in town, but she kept the trailer park and her personal account at Bank Daddy's. She had seen him many times while making deposits, but had never spoken to him. She had never taken her son to the bank. Today would be a different type of visit.

Eula walked right past his receptionist and straight into his office. Mr. Morgan looked up as she closed the door. The receptionist flew in to extract Eula. With eyes and mouth wide open in disbelief, she apologized to her boss for allowing the intrusion, but he waved her off.

"It's all right, Mary. I'll call you if I need anything."

Mr. Morgan had stood abruptly when Eula entered his office. After Mary closed the door, he remained standing for a moment before sitting down again.

Eula had already taken a seat on the other side of his massive cherry wood desk.

He had no idea why, after all these years, she had decided to confront him in person, entering his office in such a brash fashion. There was a moment of nervousness on both sides of the desk. Eula found herself, momentarily, at a loss for words. Glancing down and seeing the flyers in her hand gave her the initiative to begin the conversation.

"I need, or I should say, we need your help with something. I'm sure you're aware the furniture plant has closed its doors for good. Most of the boys who worked there are my friends. They'll find jobs in the city, but for right now, they're a little short of cash and Christmas is bearing down on them like a mother grizzly protecting her cubs."

Mr. Morgan, shifting his weight in his huge leather chair, covered his mouth to stifle a yawn, pretended or real.

"We've decided to have a tour of the homes at the trailer park, much like the tour of homes the town has each year. It would solve the immediate financial crisis, and might just give the trailer park residents and the folk who live in town a chance to meet, and who knows, find out they might have something in common."

"And just how do I fit into this picture," Mr. Morgan asked.

Handing him a big stack of flyers, Eula said, "Make it happen."

"There's no way I'm going to pass out these flyers, or put any pressure on any of my friends or customers to visit your trailer park, let alone pay to do it. I don't want this bank, or my good name, associated with you or anyone else in that trailer park."

"I figured that would be your response," Eula said as she stood to leave.

"I had a deal with your father and paid a premium to make you and your kind go away. I'm under no obligation to do anything for you, or your boys, this Christmas, or any Christmas, for that matter."

Eula leaned over and put both hands on his desk.

"My father's dead," she said softly, "and your good name would look tarnished next to his, so please refrain from ever mentioning my father again. This is not about any obligation you owe me. This is about doing the right thing because you can, that's all."

Eula started for the door and Mr. Morgan stood up and said, "Here, take your flyers with you."

Pausing and turning to face him, Eula said, "Would you like for me to tell the town about Sue Ellen, or would you prefer to give the good ol boys a little endorsement about our upcoming tour. You decide. If it's the latter, please be at my office, that's my office in the trailer park, at 9 AM in the morning. And Bank Daddy, don't be late."

She had a sudden impulse to slam the door behind her, but

thought better of it. She never dreamed she would've called him Bank Daddy to his face. Kinda slipped out, but it sure felt good. He didn't follow, which told her she'd better get home and clean up her office for their meeting. She winked at the receptionist as she passed by her desk.

Bubba and the boys loved the flyers. They still doubted if any hootie tooties would actually come to the trailer park, let alone pay to come inside their homes. But Eula knew better. Two words gave her all the confidence in the world that this would be a huge success—Sue Ellen.

She was a little disappointed in the boys. They weren't the least bit interested in getting started on the clean-up or the decorations. She knew they felt the difference money made in the scheme of things, but she knew there was actually more rejection on the part of the trailer park residents than on the part of the townspeople. They would never admit it, but Bubba and the boys were far more likely to snub the townsfolk than the other way around. After all, Eula had first-hand experience. William had not only fathered her son, but was still very much in love with her and was a very significant part of their lives.

It was time to have a come-to-Jesus meeting. She dispersed the boys to every trailer with an announcement of a very special meeting to begin in one hour at her office.

Thankfully the weather was exceptionally mild and in just a little while, seventy-five residents had assembled, eager to hear what Eula had to say.

She laid it on hard and thick.

"It's now just twenty- two days until Christmas. I've come up with a great idea to make an exceptional amount of money for the Holiday Season. I must have complete cooperation in order to make this tour of homes a success. If we do well, we'll do it every year. But you have to do your part. Y'all get together and decide which homes you want to showcase. I think we should do eight—four doublewides and four singlewides. I want this place shining like new money, and I want the homes you select to be decorated to the best of your ability. I have garland for the split rail fence out front, and I'll buy more so we can decorate the fence down by the pavilion."

Eula paused, took a deep breath, and then continued.

"Some of you boys go out and get the largest cedar tree you can find and let's put it up at the entrance. There's some nice ones down by High Shoals Creek, and old Mr. Riley won't care if you cut one. I'll call and tell him y'all are coming. Bubba will select a grill committee to cook the dogs and burgers. I'll buy all the fixings and beer."

Bubba caught Eula looking directly at him; he smiled and she winked. She sounded like a drill sergeant, barking orders to new recruits.

"Set the refreshments up under the pavilion. Get the washtubs out of the storage shed. They'll add a trailer park touch and will be a great way to ice down the beer. Pray for good weather, but at least we have the pavilion if the weather doesn't cooperate. We'll have a bonfire. The cooler the weather, the larger the fire. The residents were spellbound, but Eula could tell she had rallied the troops around the cause—their cause.

"One more thing and I'll hush. Mama used to say, 'be yourself, but don't forget your raising.' Y'all are the best, and this will be a great time, not just to showcase our trailer park, but to showcase how our Mamas raised us. Any questions?"

"Only one," Clarice said timidly. "Bubba says no one from town will come out here to see our homes and how we live. What if nobody shows up?"

"Here's what y'all need to know. At 9 AM in the morning, Mr. William Morgan, president of First City Bank, will drive down this driveway and stop at my office to discuss his part in making this a huge success. He already has a stack of flyers on his desk and is eager to help."

"Wow," Little Jimmy said. "How'd you pull that one off?"

"We probably don't want to know," Bubba said. The entire group broke into laughter.

"You probably don't," Eula responded and laughed as well.

"You're all standing around here like you're raring to go and can't go for raring. Get out of here and get to work. Let's have this place looking good before Mr. Morgan gets here in the morning."

They scattered quickly and seemed energized and ready to make it happen. Bubba was the only one who didn't leave.

"You must have pulled out a pretty big trump card," he said with a somber tone in his voice. "I won't let you down. I have my doubts about this, but I have faith in you. What about The Beast? Think those hootie tooties would like a ride in the beast?"

The beast was a monster pickup truck one of the residents had built from scratch. He used it to climb over cars and to compete in mud-bogging events. You had to use a ladder to get in the cab.

"That's a great idea," Eula said. "That's what I'm talking about. Can you imagine how excited some of those guys in town would be to ride in or drive the beast? They see y'all driving it and wonder why. But, what if they could drive it? Wow! What a touch that would add to the tour."

Eula started to go inside her office.

"Bubba, you got a minute? Come inside and let's have a beer. We need to talk."

Her tone was a little disconcerting. It sounded motherly, and sad, all at the same time. She returned from her fridge and handed Bubba a beer. Pulling the tab, she took a long draw from the can, and then sat down hard. Bubba was almost afraid to pull the tab on his beer. This sounded very serious, and reminded him of being in the principal's office.

"Do you mind if I call you Tom?" she asked.

"Not at all. No one ever calls me Tom anymore. I'm just Bubba to everyone."

"Exactly," Eula agreed, "but for this conversation, I need you to be Tom, not Bubba. Okay?"

"Okay," Bubba said as he sat down in a chair opposite Eula.

"I'm smart, Tom, but so are you. In high school we hung out with our kind, or at least what we perceived was our kind. Most of the time, kind was defined by money, cars, and homes. We knew who we were, and more importantly, we knew who they were. But, Tom, we were so wrong." She paused, as if collecting her thoughts, and Bubba finally pulled the tab on his beer. "We were guilty of building the fences which separated us, not them. We like to remember our experiences as being extras on a movie set, with the others being the stars. That wasn't the case. They're not hootie tooties as you jokingly call them. While some may use money and possessions to make them feel superior, the vast majority of folks who have money are great people, and will befriend anyone who is open to their friendship."

"Where's this all going, and what does it have to do with now? That was a long time ago, or at least it seems like it was."

"I have a secret to share with you, Tom. My William is like that. He loves people and doesn't see money and position as tools to separate himself from some who might have less."

"Your William, as in the William who's your son's father?"

"Here's the secret I'm going to trust you with. No one else knows about it. I see William on a regular basis. He loved me in high school and still does. The feelings are mutual. He hasn't married, and you know I haven't either. Though he's not directly involved in Billy's life, he pays the tuition for his private school and the headmaster knows to contact William in case there is an emergency and the school can't reach me. I have arranged it so William will have custody in case something should happen to me. His father is one of those people who make money their god and uses it to isolate himself from those with less of the world's goods. He's a hard man, and my prayer is that one day, William will be able to stand up to his father."

"Wow!" was all Bubba could muster.

"I need to ask you for a favor. I need you to be Bubba to your friends, and especially Bubba to our visitors who'll be coming to tour our homes. But, for just a little while, I need you to be Tom for me. Do you understand what I'm asking and why?"

"You know I do. It's a whole lot easier to be Bubba than to be Tom.

But for you, Tom will leave your office, but Bubba will go to work. And, thanks for telling me about William. It's a great love story, but a sad story as well. Tom would cry, but Bubba won't let him."

Eula laughed a hearty laugh, finished her beer, crushed the can, and shot a two-pointer in her waste basket across the room.

"William's a lucky man," Tom said as Bubba left her office.

He knew what she needed him to do. Not be Bubba or Tom, but a little of each. Assembling his friends, he gave them a speech of his own, declaring his utmost confidence in Eula's idea. After delegating jobs to each one, he began laying out a course for the Beast. The wives of the selected tour homes were busy cleaning and decorating. There was a hum of activity in the trailer park he had never witnessed before. Little Jimmy was singing Christmas carols as he strung the garland on the split rail fence.

That night, Eula had a hard time going to sleep. Just like Bubba, she hid behind a tough, *I don't give a damn,* exterior. But inside, in the recesses of her soul, she was caring and vulnerable. Why else would she wait, pray, and hope one day William would find the courage to stand up to his father. She could marry any number of available men in town but she loved only William.

"Would Mr. Morgan show up in the morning?" she asked herself while staring at the clock next to her bed. "Listen to me," she scolded herself. "I gave Bubba all this advice on building fences between ourselves and others, and I'm the architect of a fence which should have been torn down years ago. Hypocrite," she said out loud.

Acknowledging shortcomings and wrongdoings is the beginning of reconciliation, and also an aid to good sleep.

Eula got up early, dressed, and was in her office by 8:30; at 8:50, still no Mr. Morgan. She was about to second-guess her privileged information when a new black Caddie pulled up in front of her office. It was Mr. Morgan in the flesh. Eula knew every eye in the trailer park had seen his arrival. With reluctance, which was visible on his face, he got out of the car and came up the steps to her office door.

Again, forgetting the advice she had given Bubba and her own self-introspection the night before, she threw up a fence of her own and changed into a genuine hootie tootie.

"Have a seat," she said, pointing to an empty chair in front of her cluttered desk.

For several minutes, Eula added up columns of meaningless figures, in an attempt to belittle the uncomfortable figure sitting in front of her. She knew it was so wrong, but enjoyed it immensely. Finally, laying the paperwork aside, she picked up a flyer for the tour and addressed him..

"Mr. Morgan, thanks for coming. With your endorsement, our tour will be very successful, and I want to tell you in advance how much we appreciate it."

"Let's just get on with your demands, sorry about that, your requests, and tell me what I have to do for my world to remain unchanged. I can't imagine where you get your intel, but I'm sure you'll protect your sources. So, tell me, how can I help?"

"It's really pretty simple. My mother used to tell me to be honest and forthright in all my dealings with others, and I've found it to be good advice. While the families in the trailer park are in a Christmas pinch, if you will, they still have pride and aren't looking for charity. We don't want any money unless we feel like we can give something back in return, hence our tour of homes. We have planned to showcase eight homes, and to have all the beer, dogs, and burgers anyone cares to consume. We'll have trailer park horseshoes, and anyone with a valid driver's license can have the thrill of a lifetime, either driving or riding in the Beast."

Mr. Morgan didn't know, or want to know, what the Beast was. He simply wanted to be out of Eula's office and back in his.

"I will, as a special favor to you, and to the residents of the trailer park, encourage all the country club members and all the Chamber members, to attend this most gala event. I won't mention the reason for the tour, but only that perhaps it's time the two parts of the city came together in unity, and in the spirit the Christmas season brings to one and all. And I'll make the flyers available at every teller window in the bank, and also in the three branch locations."

"Very well put," Eula noted, "and I personally want to extend an invitation to you to be our guest of honor. I think it'll show sincerity, and will help to solidify two distinct segments of our community, showing how little where we live defines who we actually are."

"Very well said, also," Mr. Morgan noted as he stood to leave. "I must be getting back to the bank. I look forward to coming back on the 14th, and I'm sure everyone attending will have something to remember well past the Christmas Season."

Eula wasn't sure "what something to remember well past the Christmas Season" meant.

Driving out of the trailer park, Mr. Morgan couldn't help but reflect on the fact Eula was well-mannered and articulate, not at all what he imagined her to be like.

Mr. Morgan, Bubba, and the residents of the park didn't know Eula had been taking on-line classes for three years and would soon graduate with a four- year degree in accounting. William had insisted she take the courses and had gladly paid her tuition.

When the Caddie was out of sight, the office was swamped by curious residents, with Bubba arriving first.

Eula, who had worried herself to death about whether Mr. Morgan would show, was cool under fire.

"How did it go," Bubba asked. "is he helping or not?"

"Went fine" she said almost absentmindedly, "just like I knew it would. And, of course, he's willing to help us any way he can. He's coming as my special guest, and I may take him for a ride in the Beast."

Once again, "Wow" was all Bubba could muster.

The residents were now both pumped and frightened. Eula had delivered the bank president to the trailer park, just like she promised. They rolled up their sleeves and went to work harder than ever, getting the park ready for the tour of homes. People living in very expensive homes and neighborhoods were about to descend upon Eula's Trailer Park for tours of eight of their best homes. While people from both sides of the tracks put their pants on the same way, the closets those pants hang in are light years apart on an economic scale. That was the only part that concerned them—could they actually connect with each other?

Eula wasn't worried about the tour. She knew people, because after all, the father of her son happened to be the son of the bank president. And, in spite of their social differences, they were attracted to each other in high school and were still in love with each other years later. The social differences loomed larger than life when it came to marriage. William lacked the courage to face his father on the issue of marrying a local girl who owned a trailer park.

By December 12th the park had been transformed into a thing of beauty. Every single aspect of the park and every single family living there was ready to entertain the townfolk. Extra grills had been borrowed from friends, and provisions were ready for a feast.

Bubba and some of the residents had laid out a course on the back acreage adjacent to the park. The Beast had been gussied up and even had twelve-volt Christmas lights around the cab that twinkled when she was running. Bubba got his friend, Ace, who owned a junk yard, to bring over three old clunkers for the Beast to climb over. A mud bog to die for was also out back across from the clunkers.

Eula prayed for good weather, and her prayers were answered. It was a mild December day, and only a light wind breaker was needed. Seems like even God wanted these two groups to find common ground. It was to be an all-day event, starting at 10 A.M. and ending with a bonfire and marsh-mellow roast.

Bubba selected a number of residents, mostly forced, to lead the tours. Eula made up an outline for the tour guides, and they rehearsed it at least a hundred times. She stressed over and over for them to just be themselves, and to embrace their visitors as they would any friend or family member. Little Jimmy pointed out none of his friends, or family members, drove fancy cars, lived in nice homes, or had money. Eula told him to pretend they did.

Eula was surprised on December 13th when Mr. Morgan called her. Hearing his voice, she expected bad news. It was great news and terrible news at the same time. He told her to expect over four hundred people to tour the park, perhaps more. Everyone was coming. As she pondered the phone call and the number of people coming, she had "Bubba" thoughts cross her mind. They had probably always wondered what those trailer park people were like and were willing to pay thirty bucks to find out and sneak a peep inside their trailers. Bubba walked in about the time she finished her negative thoughts, picked up on her countenance and asked, "Are you having a Bubba moment, or a Tom moment?"

"Both," she told him and laughed. "Guess what? Mr. Morgan just called and said about two hundred people might come for the tour."

Bubba about had a fit.

"You gotta be kidding me," he said. "Two hundred! Wow!"

Eula knew better than to give him the real numbers. He might saddle up the Beast and ride away for good.

On the morning of the 14th, cars started lining up early. It was evident curiosity was a driving force, second only to Bank Daddy burning up a lot of capital. At first, Bubba and the tour guides were a little reluctant to let their hair down and be themselves. But the genuine friendliness of the residents and the beautifully decorated trailer homes soon won everyone's heart. The burgers and dogs were to die for, and the trailer park horseshoes went over better than tickets to the Masters. People weren't leaving fast enough, and soon the county Sheriff's department had half their force out there trying to direct traffic.

And the Beast! What can we say about the Beast? Grown men became little boys again, and it was really Christmas in a new and different way for most of the townsfolk. The big, ugly, misunderstood truck had a personality all its own.

Mr. Morgan arrived as promised and came to Eula's office for his special guided tour.

"I don't know what's happened here today, but those coming

back to town are so excited about making so many new friends. I think they realize, some for the first time, money and possessions often possess much more than they're possessed. They've met a great bunch of people, who have so much less of the world's goods, and yet own so much more of its happiness."

Eula was visibly shaken by his honesty. Her eyes were full of tears. She told him it was her turn.

"Christmas brings out the best in all of us," she began. "I want to ask you to forgive me for harboring so much animosity toward you over these past few years. I don't know why you did what you did back then, and truth is, I might have done the same thing if I had been in your shoes. There's so much I'd like to tell you, but it's not my place. Let's you and me go meet some really nice people, who, like the towns-folk, have made some really great friends today. And when the tour is over, I'm going to take you on the ride of a life time. Disney has nothing on us."

After the tour, Eula and Mr. Morgan stopped by the grill for a Bubba burger. They were about to go find the Beast when Eula received the shock of her life. She stood up so quickly, she startled Mr. Morgan.

"Mother," she heard her son calling, as he ran toward the pavilion. William was right behind him.

"Mother, this really nice man picked me up at school and brought me home in a really neat Corvette."

Mr. Morgan also stood up, turned around, and saw the boy running toward them. William smiled at his dad.

Eula hugged her little Billy and said, "Son, this really nice man is your father, and this really nice man here is your grandfather."

William didn't miss a beat as he took Eula's hand and said, "Dad, may I introduce you to my soon-to-be wife?"

"Wow," was all Mr. Morgan could say.

Epilogue

Things were never the same again. City Bank now sponsors not one, but two annual Christmas Tour of Homes. Eula's Trailer Park is by far the most popular. The number of Beasts have grown considerably and find themselves parked by some very expensive residences. Hootie Tootie has disappeared from the vernacular. Bubba went to technical school and now has a successful heating and air conditioning business; Tom's HVAC. He employs a lot of his friends. Six of the richest people in town sold their massive homes and bought doublewides. They swear they've never been happier. William and Eula now have four children and live in a very modest home. Little Jimmy and his wife manage the trailer park.

Grandpa Morgan gave up his job at the bank. Four grandchildren keep him plenty busy. Eula heard through the grapevine Sue Ellen passed away, taking a dark secret to her grave.

The God of the manor house is also the God of the trailer park, and all the people therein belong to Him. Amen and Amen.

ABOUT THE AUTHOR

Gene Vickers lives in Young Harris, GA. He has been married to Elaine for 56 years and they have two children and seven grandchildren. He has been in the fire protection business for fifty-four years. Writing is his hobby and he's especially partial to short stories and flash fiction. Vickers looks forward to retiring so he can devote more time to writing. He says life is full of short stories and all one has to do is look around to see them. His last published work, *Amen and Amen,* was awarded The Silver Book Award by Literary Titan. This is his third book.

Other Books by Gene Vickers

Imagine This

Amen and Amen

www.ingramcontent.com/pod-product-compliance
Lightning Source LLC
Chambersburg PA
CBHW070547100726
47907CB00004B/1304

9781665300957